The Interracial Adoption Option

THE Interracial Adoption *Option*

Creating a Family Across Race

Marlene G. Fine and Fern L. Johnson

Jessica Kingsley *Publishers*
London and Philadelphia

First published in 2013
by Jessica Kingsley Publishers
73 Collier Street
London N1 9BE, UK
and
400 Market Street, Suite 400
Philadelphia, PA 19106, USA

www.jkp.com

Library of Congress Cataloging in Publication Data
Fine, Marlene Gail, 1949-
 The interracial adoption option : creating a family across race / Marlene G. Fine and Fern L. Johnson.
    pages cm
 Includes bibliographical references and index.
 ISBN 978-1-84905-930-5 (alk. paper)
 1. Interracial adoption. 2. Adoption--Psychological aspects. 3. Identity (Psychology) 4. Families. I.
Johnson, Fern L. II. Title.
 HV875.6.F56 2013
 306.874--dc23
                                    2013000290

British Library Cataloguing in Publication Data
A CIP catalogue record for this book is available from the British Library

ISBN 978 1 84905 930 5
eISBN 978 0 85700 717 9

Printed and bound in the United States

For William and Julius, and the teens and young adults who have grown up with them in our adoption group.

Contents

ACKNOWLEDGMENTS   9

Introduction   11

1. Making the Decision to Adopt a Child of
Another Race—*When Birds of a Feather
Might Not Flock Together*   17

2. Talking about Race and Adoption—*"You're
Doing What?!"*   47

3. Helping Your Child Develop a Healthy Racial
Identity—*"Daddy, Why Am I Brown and You're Pink?"* 71

4. Talking about Race and Adoption with Your
Child—*"Mommy, Who's My Real Daddy?"*   99

5. Navigating School—*Homework for Parents*   *121*

6. Creating a Support System for You and Your
Child—*"It Takes a Village"*   149

INDEX   163

Acknowledgments

It does take a village. So many people helped us on our journey and provided encouragement and support as we worked on this book. We asked a number of people to read draft chapters as we completed them. Their comments were validating and also valuable in offering perspectives we had not thought of, clarifying points, and offering suggestions for resources. To those who took the time for this type of review, we are enormously grateful: Susan Beaton, Julia Demmin, Jim Gomes, Daryl Hellman, D'Lynn Jacobs, Mary Ann LaRoche, Dave Logan, Alex Mikulich, Kathleen Reardon, Sue Roberts, Nancy Schroeder, Brad Seamans, and Larry Seamans.

We are also grateful for friends and colleagues who have supported us throughout our adoption journey. Some were there at the very beginning and others later, but all embraced and supported our family: Betsy Astolfi, Doug Astolfi, Beverly Baccelli, Gary Bailey, Roy Bellush, Lois Brynes, Susan Copeland, Gail Dines, Christy Egun, Serena Hilsinger, Marsha Houston, Betsy Huang, Esther Jones, Fatali Karimi, Jayne Karimi, David Levy, Carol Owen, Tony Nixon, Pearl Peters, Janet Rickles, Marge Ropp, Paul Ropp, Charlena Seymour, Harry Seymour, Ruth Sharpe, Dick Traina (now deceased), Polly Traina, Arthur Young, and Frank Waldorf.

Steve Jones, our editor at JKP, was enthusiastic about our proposal and confident that we could write this book. We thank him for his interest in our work and for making everything move smoothly along the way. Everyone at JKP was helpful and prompt in answering all of our many questions. We especially thank Carolyn Holleyman, Sarah Hull, and Victoria Nicholas for their careful and supportive assistance during the various production stages of the book.

Finally, we could not have made this journey without the love and participation of our families: Marlene's parents, Fred (now deceased) and Lillian Fine; Fern's mother, Clara Johnson (now deceased); and Fern's siblings and their families. We are especially indebted to Mary and Ben Ho, Fern's sister and brother-in-law, for being the greatest aunt and uncle imaginable. "Auntie Mary" was there every step of the way, including flying to Massachusetts from Minnesota to take care of our children while we attended professional conferences. Our sons, William and Julius, are the center of this story. They too read draft chapters, and they listened patiently to our endless questions and "thinking out loud" about the book. We are so proud of how they have carried the challenges of their identities and so immensely happy that they came into our lives.

Introduction

We parked in front of the small house on a quiet street in a place we had been to once before. We sat talking, nervously wondering if we were doing the right thing. We had been together for 14 years and had a two-year-old adopted son. Could we possibly love another child as much as we loved him? We had come to this same house exactly two years before to meet our baby son, who, at four weeks old, was a gorgeous child—smiling and alert, with enormous brown eyes and impossibly long black eyelashes. He had grown into a happy, active, loving two-year-old, adored by his parents and everyone else in his life. Now we were about to adopt our second child, another boy who was described as having dreamy brown eyes and cocoa-colored skin.

We both finally took a deep breath and walked to the front door. When the social worker brought the baby—*our baby*—downstairs and put him in Fern's arms, any lingering doubts disappeared. His eyes were, indeed, as dreamy as we had been told, his little body soft and receptive, and we instantly knew he would be loved.

The story of our family began many years before this moment. It is a love story of family, friends, and community. And it is a story that we want to share in the hope that it will encourage others to be open to adopting a child, and especially to adopting one of the thousands of children of color in the

U.S. and throughout the world who are waiting for families. If you are considering adoption and are white, we also hope that our story will help you decide if parenting a child of color is right for you. Our experience has been joyful and rewarding beyond measure, as we believe parenting is for most people. It has also been challenging, as we believe parenting also is for most people. We have learned a lot along the way about not only ourselves and our children, but also the culture we live in here in the U.S. Our own story and the stories of the many people we have met over the years who took similar journeys are the foundation for this book. In the chapters that follow, we offer you what we have learned, and hope that you will learn from it also. In many ways, the book is a response to what we did *not* have when we started the interracial adoption process. We did not have an overview to help us think through the many questions flooding our minds. We found many resources and individuals to help us with the adoption process. But interracial adoption? Not so much.

We have titled the book *The Interracial Adoption Option: Creating a Family Across Race* because we want to draw attention to the complex nature of race and how it affects adoption. It has not been our intent to write this book as an argument for why white people should adopt children of color. There are reasons for and against interracial adoption. For those who want to adopt, the decision-making process is personal. Our only bias in this process is that we think the decision-making process is enriched through openness to adopting outside of one's racial group. As our society's diversity increases, the oddness of interracial adoption will likely be replaced by greater acceptance and expectation that families will be diverse. Today we see more interracial dating and marriage than ever before, and this trend is likely to continue. We hope that over time, racial differences within families will not be that unusual and that the attitudes and experiences of the younger generations will soften the racial divide that still exists in so many places.

The book is divided into six chapters, with each chapter dealing with a significant topic related to interracial adoption. We take you from making the decision to adopt a child of another race through the many challenges in helping your child develop a healthy racial identity as he or she grows up. We look at social and cultural issues that shape our understanding of race, our talk about race, and our behaviors in response to racial issues. And we provide practical advice about talking with others about what you're doing, deciding where to live, talking with your child's teachers, and taking care of your child's hair and skin. We do not claim to have covered everything of importance to the process of interracial adoption in this book, nor do we claim that each topic is covered thoroughly. We want this book to be a starting point and a springboard for deeper reflection and research that will be helpful in both making the decision about interracial adoption and dealing with issues and situations that are sure to arise once you become a multiracial family through adoption.

The book's organization makes sense to us as a sequence of significant considerations, but not necessarily as a chronology of how experiences occur over time. If you read the chapters in order, the references we make to things we have discussed previously will make sense, which is one way we intertwine the chapters in the order in which we present them. We have, however, written each chapter with the thought in mind that a reader might be interested in sampling from them or rearranging how they are read, or perhaps skimming some and reading others more carefully.

We draw from many experiences we have had in our family over more than two decades and from an amalgam of reading and conversations with a broad range of people. The chapters are not laden with references, although we do include relevant material that helped us think about the topics we discuss and that might be useful to follow up on for those who are interested. After the main discussion we provide a list of "Thing to consider." At the end of each chapter, in addition to the references, we list a few additional resources that either illustrate topics in the chapter or deal with them in greater depth.

Our adopted children are African American and the main focus of this book is on white people adopting black children. We believe, though, that our experiences will be relevant and valuable to anyone who is thinking about adopting or has adopted a child of a different race. Adopting a child of Asian or Hispanic background, for example, will not involve the exact same cultural issues as adopting a black child. White parents who adopt a child of another race will encounter and have to deal with different social perceptions, expectations, and stereotypes depending on the identity category in which the child is placed. Yet, all white parents who create multiracial families through adoption have the same responsibility to actively engage a range of cultural assumptions at work every day in our society that are often out of the awareness of most white people (the two of us included). The assumptions range from those about the definition of a family to the identity of adopted children to the deeply embedded ideas about what it means to be one race or another, one ethnicity or another. To make these connections explicit, we have integrated examples from different ancestry backgrounds into the book. Although we have not included information or examples from countries other than the United States, we believe that many of the experiences we had as white parents of black children in the U.S. are relevant to anyone adopting a child of a different race anywhere in the world.

The terms we use throughout the book are not technical but nonetheless require some clarification. *Interracial* adoption refers to placing a child of one racial or ethnic group with adoptive parents of another. The term *transracial* is often used to refer to the same concept in the literature on interracial adoption. We use *interracial* in the title of the book, but also use *transracial* at times throughout the text. *Race* itself is a complicated term—not just because it is a culturally arbitrary and history-laden category (an issue that we begin to talk about in Chapter 1 and continue to explore throughout the book) but also because there are technical definitions that come into play when we are looking at statistics. The U.S. Bureau of the Census defines population groups on the basis of race. In the 2010 census, there were 15 options provided for responding to the questions about race: White, Black or African American, American Indian and Alaska Native, seven different Asian groups (Asian Indian, Chinese, Filipino, Japanese, Korean, Vietnamese, Other Asian), Native Hawaiian, Samoan, Guamanian or Chamorro, Other Pacific Islander, and Some Other Race. Respondents could check one or more of these categories. Very often when we read reports about race or hear it mentioned in the news, these categories are collapsed into black, white, and Asian—often leaving out American Indian and all the specific Asian and Pacific Islander groups. Many people, for example, do not think of those from India as "Asian," but they are definitely included in this census grouping.

Ethnicity is another complex term that we use in the book. Ethnicity is confusing because it is sometimes defined as characteristic of human groups that have racial, religious, linguistic, and certain other traits in common. The inclusion of race in the list of shared traits often leads people to use race and ethnicity interchangeably. The census, however, distinguishes between race and ethnicity, asking each person to indicate *ethnicity* as "Hispanic" or "not Hispanic." This means that every person is counted in the census by both racial category and whether or not the person is Hispanic. A Hispanic person could be either white or black (or Asian or another racial category, although white and black are the races most commonly found in Hispanic cultures), and the U.S. Bureau of the Census sorts data in this way. We prefer to use ethnicity in the way that is implied by the census categories: as a term that denotes the cultural traditions of a group of people. In other words, ethnicity has to do with sociological factors rather than physical characteristics. We stress, however, that these terms are arbitrary and completely culture-bound. Americans see race and ethnicity in certain ways because of historical practices and conventional language usage. Terms also change over time, as clearly shown by changes in 20th-century usage from "colored" to "negro" to "African American" and "black." "People of color" is also a relatively new term, and we use it to designate all non-white people. In the educational process, we often refer to "race and ethnicity" to signal population factors and social issues that are present for those groups not in the white majority. However, as you will see in Chapter 3 when we talk about African American culture, even that definition becomes problematic in distinguishing race and ethnicity.

Added to this array of possibilities are *biracial, multiracial,* and *mixed race.* There are no exact meanings for these terms, but we think it's important to point out that claiming these as identity terms is personal to the individual involved. When part of the bi- or multi- of mixed race is "white," those who are white need to be cautious in assuming that the "white" part weighs equally with the other parts for those involved. This is especially important in understanding how children of mixed racial background raised by white parents are labeled by other people, and how they experience their racial identities.

Finally, we have chosen not to capitalize the word *black* when referring to a population group because the term is elastic across different national origins, sometimes referring to African Americans and other times to racial identities outside the United States. We do capitalize *Asian* because the term is drawn from a continent, and the convention in the English language is to capitalize continents. Similarly, "Latino/a" is derived from "Latin America" and "Latin American."

Our hope is that *The Interracial Adoption Option* will be a helpful introduction to the topic, will stimulate thinking about how families are created through adoption, and will aid in thinking through decisions to be made when thinking about adoption options and other decisions for multiracial families created through adoption. Race remains one of the most complex aspects of our society and, when mixed with adoption, implies a distinctive journey in creating a family.

CHAPTER 1

Making the Decision to Adopt a Child of Another Race—

When Birds of a Feather Might Not Flock Together

We decided to adopt a child in August 1987. We were sitting on the beach in Pesaro, Italy, when we made our decision. We had come to this beach every day for a week and watched the Italian families and friends who were vacationing together "ooh" and "aah" over their children, smiling rather than screaming when the kids poured sand on the neatly arranged beach chairs, running after the little ones who wandered too far into the sea, all participating in the communal care and adoration of the children. We were struck by how the Italians seemed to love children unconditionally, without trying to discipline them into adult behavior, and how family and friends together took responsibility for watching out for them in a much more relaxed way than is usually the case in the U.S. Simultaneously we voiced the same thought to each other—"We could have a family if we could raise our children like that rather than the way most Americans seem to raise their children." And so we began to discuss the possibility of adopting a child. Of course we eventually raised our children in some of the same ways our parents raised us and our friends were raising their children—in a nuclear family with the usual erratic forms of American discipline—but that's another story.

When we returned to the U.S. and began to explore adoption, we discovered a mostly subterranean world. As academics, we looked first for books and articles to guide us. We found few. We then asked friends if they knew people who had recently adopted. We even tracked down people we read about in the newspaper who were identified as having adopted children and contacted them, asking if they would be willing to talk to us about their experiences. After a few phone calls to various adoption agencies, it was clear that, unless we wanted to wait eight to ten years, our options were to adopt a child from outside the U.S. or a child of color from the U.S. Fern's sister-in-law is Korean and Fern's family is Lutheran (the Lutheran church at that time was closely tied to the adoption of Korean children), so we first explored adopting a Korean child. As two single women seeking to adopt (lesbian and gay adoption was not yet legal in Massachusetts), we were automatically excluded from adopting a Korean child because the Korean government required adoptive parents be married. Fern's sister-in-law then suggested that she find a Korean child in Guam, where she and Fern's brother were living at the time, but we were uncertain whether we could pursue that option. Our next possibility was the Philippines, but the law there was even more restrictive than Korea: adoptive parents needed to be married and Catholic. India was next on our list because we knew one person who had adopted a girl from there, but we discovered that babies adopted from India at that time often had cerebral palsy. We learned that girl babies in India are not highly valued, so when a woman learned she was expecting a girl and decided to put the child up for adoption, doctors often induced birth early, which increased the likelihood that the baby would be born with cerebral palsy. We knew we couldn't handle a child with a serious birth defect, so we crossed India off our list. Then we explored various options in Latin and South America. Colombia seemed a good choice until they shut down foreign adoptions. We were also nervous about the stories we had heard of babies being stolen from their birth mothers and sold for adoption in Colombia. Finally, we learned that single women could adopt from Peru— as long as the potential adoptive parent went to Peru to live for six months. Although neither of us was fluent in Spanish, Fern was due for a sabbatical from her university, and we seriously considered moving to Peru for six months.

At the same time as we were researching international adoption, we began the actual adoption process by signing up with an adoption agency specializing in international adoption and starting a home study. Because we had to apply as single women, we started two separate processes. Each of us completed a long application form that included questions about the kind of child we wanted to adopt. This seemed strange at first, until we realized that adoption agencies did everything possible to avoid placements that would not be successful. Would we adopt a child of another race? A child from another country? An older child? A child with physical disabilities? A child whose developmental prognosis was questionable? A child with an illness? We were both very clear in answering these questions. We wanted a physically healthy child who had a reasonable chance for normal physical and mental development. We preferred an infant but would be happy with a toddler. We did not want to adopt an older child. And we were open to international adoption. Race did not matter—except in the case of an African American baby. We both remember writing impassioned statements on our applications about how we respected, even though we didn't agree with, the National Association of Black Social Workers (NABSW) declaration that the adoption of African American children by whites was a form of genocide (NABSW 1972).

We concluded, therefore, that we would not adopt an African American child in deference to the NABSW's position. (The NABSW has since modified its position, see NABSW 2003.)

Fern's application went more quickly and she started group sessions about adoption. One evening she returned home from a session and said we needed to talk. The topic for that session was domestic adoption of children of color. The social worker who was leading the discussion began by saying that she understood if people in the group had decided not to adopt a black child because of personal reasons, but that if their decision was based on the belief that a black child would be better served being raised by a black family (or black single parent), they should consider the statistics on the adoption of black children. Although blacks in the U.S. are somewhat more likely to be interested in adoption than whites, they often face structural barriers to being approved for adoption (see Chapter 4). The result is that there are simply not enough black families available for the large number of black children waiting to be adopted. That means that large numbers of black children end up spending their lives in foster care, becoming less likely to be adopted with each passing year. So the real choice was not between a black child being raised by a black family or a white family, but rather between a black child having a family or being shuttled through the foster care system. That night, we began to rethink our decision to adopt a child from another country. And for the first time, we confronted the hypocrisy of our position that it was okay to parent a child of a different race born outside of the U.S. but not a child of a different race born here.

By morning we had decided to amend our original applications to state that our first choice was an African American or mixed-race child from the U.S. Given the large number of African American babies and children waiting for an adoption placement, we were told that the process would now begin to move quickly and we needed to be prepared. Not just for the arrival of a baby in our lives, but also for having an African

American baby and for confronting our attitudes and beliefs about race. Both of us are academics who specialize in issues related to race, racial identity, and interracial communication. Our academic knowledge gave us a foundation but we understood we needed to learn more. We didn't understand, however, just how much more.

Two experiences immediately after we made our decision made painfully clear to us how little we knew about and understood racial attitudes and their pervasiveness in American life. The first was a visit to see friends who had recently adopted an African American infant. The baby was relatively dark skinned (black babies have lighter skin tones that usually darken as the child gets older). That evening we had an intense conversation about skin color. We wondered if a child would prefer to have skin closer in color to ours. And the darkness of the baby's skin forced us to confront our own hidden prejudices—how dark was too dark? What does "too dark" mean? Was a light colored African American child preferable? How could we even think that? By morning we had agreed that we didn't care what color our child would be. But we were shaken to realize that we had cared about skin color for that brief moment and had actually thought there might be a legitimate reason to think about shades of darkness. We weren't so naïve as to assume that skin color wouldn't be an issue for our child, but we were naïve in assuming that we were immune from prejudice and the kind of naïvety that made us think about degrees of similarity to us *as white people.*

The second experience occurred a few days later when Marlene called her parents to tell them about our decision to adopt an African American child. Her parents had been very supportive of our decision to adopt a child from a foreign country and were excited about the prospect of welcoming their first grandchild. Marlene grew up in a politically liberal family and her parents had always taught their children to treat people of all races, religions, and social classes as equals. So she was shocked when her mother responded to the news by insisting that we were making a mistake because "birds of a feather should flock together" (yes, she actually said that). Marlene quickly pulled herself together and replied that we were adopting a child for ourselves and not for our families, and that she hoped her parents would have the experience of being grandparents to that child, but the choice was theirs. We had made our choice. Then she hung up. Her mother called back within a few minutes and apologized for her comments. But her immediate response was another reminder of the deeply held feelings Americans have about race. And a reminder that, as Cornel West (1993) says, "race matters."

As we expected, once we notified our adoption agency that we wanted to adopt an African American baby, the process began to move quickly. We had been clear since the beginning of our search that we didn't care about the sex of our child. We wanted to be "surprised" in the same way that biological parents are when they first learn their child's sex. We also had no personal preferences about raising a boy or a girl. We were told immediately by our social worker that our decision not to specify the sex of the baby we hoped to adopt meant that we were likely to get a referral for an African American boy. "Okay, we're going to be the parents of a black boy!"

The numbers on adoption are clear—girls are in much greater demand than boys. According to the Adoption Foundation (2011), both international and domestic adoption agencies report a "strong preference" for girls, and that preference is seen across all races, socioeconomic statuses, and ages. The reasons why aren't quite as clear, but our experience with the adoption system and our conversations with social workers and prospective parents suggest that women are usually the driving force behind the decision to adopt. Most heterosexual couples come to adoption after a long process of trying to become pregnant. We have been told that at the end of that process, women are more likely than men to decide that they are willing to give up their dream of creating a family biologically if they can create one through adoption. Many men, on the other hand, appear more reluctant to consider raising a child that is not biologically their own. They agree to adopt only after their wives insist that they cannot face a future without children.

Women are also more likely to be making the decision about the sex of the child to be adopted in other potential family arrangements. Single women are much more likely to enter the adoption process than single men, just as lesbians are more likely to consider adoption than gay men. Although gender roles and expectations continue to evolve, women still have greater responsibility for child rearing, and social/cultural norms encourage women to raise children and discourage men without wives from doing so. And despite high profile parenting by gay men such as Elton John and his partner, David Furnish, Americans remain wary about having gay men raise children. So it is women who are expressing a preference about the sex of the child they are about to adopt. Most women grow up dreaming about having a little girl to nurture and love and to one day be best friends with, regardless of whether the dream is for a daughter who's "sugar and spice and everything nice" or one who will become a CEO of a Fortune 500 company. The dominant cultural belief that "men are from Mars and women from Venus" gets played out in the assumption that women are better able to understand, relate to, and talk with their daughters, while men are better equipped to raise sons because they can teach them to throw a football, hold a baseball bat, or bait a fishhook—and ultimately to perform in the competitive workplace. (By the way, we don't agree with that myth.) And since women generally make the decision to adopt, they are more likely to request a girl.

Another reason why girls are in greater demand than boys is that there is a predominant cultural belief that girls are easier to raise than boys. Our stereotypes of girls suggest that they will be sweet, docile, and helpful with domestic chores. Stereotypes of boys, on the other hand, suggest they will need a firm hand to keep them under control. Issues of control are even more salient with regard to raising black boys. Fear of black men is deeply ingrained in U.S. society and continues today, especially fear of black men by white women, so white women are not likely to request a black boy. African American women, on the other hand, are well aware of the risks black boys face in the U.S. Less than 50 percent are likely to graduate from high school, which means that they are less likely than white boys either to attend or graduate from college (Gerson 2012). The unemployment rate for black men is nearly double the rate for white men and has remained stagnant even during the recent economic recovery (Hooda 2012). One in three black men will be incarcerated at some point in his life, and more than half of black men without a high school diploma will spend time in prison by the time they are in their mid-30s (Herbert 2010). Most chilling, however, is that homicide is the leading cause of death for young black males. It would be understandable for black women to be reluctant to take on the responsibility of raising a black male child given those odds. Later in this chapter we'll discuss institutional racism, which plays a large part in these statistics.

All things considered, the reality is that black boys are rarely the child of choice for adoption. For us and many others, this meant that when we said that we didn't care about the sex of our baby, we were fairly certain that we would get a boy.

One of the requirements for adoption in Massachusetts is a home study, which is intended to demonstrate that adoptive parents have a home that meets certain standards for raising a child, for example, a separate bedroom for the child. Before we could have a home study, however, we needed to settle on a home.

Where should we live?—*"Get out the map!"*

At the time that we decided to adopt, we had our main residence in western Massachusetts, where Fern worked. Because Marlene worked in Boston, we also had a condo in Boston that Marlene used during the week. Fern was at a point in her career where it was appropriate for her to seek a new position. So she went on the job market to find a position closer to Boston, which would allow us to have one household. Within a few months Fern received an offer that made it possible for us to consolidate our living arrangements and look for a new home where we could both live within commuting distance to our jobs.

Massachusetts, like many states, has weak urban schools with diverse populations and suburbs that tend to have strong schools that are primarily white. Unless you have a lot of money to put down on a new home and a substantial income to pay the monthly mortgage, moving to the communities with the best schools is challenging. But even in the suburbs, there are wide variations in school systems. The best schools, not surprisingly, are in the wealthiest suburbs. And the wealthiest suburbs are white (we explore location and schools in greater detail in Chapter 5).

Despite its reputation as a bastion of liberalism, Massachusetts remains a highly segregated state, with people of color and immigrants found primarily in large cities. Most of the state, however, is suburban or rural, and whites are the predominant racial group in the state. But population segregation is not simply a matter of white suburbia versus diverse cities. Urban areas in the state also are segregated. Boston, for example, is divided into neighborhoods characterized by race and ethnicity—the North End is white and Italian, South Boston is white and Irish, Roxbury is African American, the Back Bay is white, Anglo-Saxon, Protestant (WASP), etc. Nearly 40 years after Boston was forced to use court-ordered busing to desegregate its schools, its neighborhoods remain stubbornly segregated. And as white families either moved their children to private schools or moved themselves to the suburbs in response to busing, the schools became increasingly black, Latino/a, and immigrant (with many of these children also in the category of English Language Learners). The net result is an urban school system starved for resources and comprising primarily students of color. Communities of color in Boston often characterize the Boston public schools, especially in reference to boys of color, as "a pipeline from school to prison," a characterization that didn't bode well for us as we considered our future family. Every state differs in exactly how race and population are distributed, but some of the same issues occur no matter where you live.

Our choices for where we should live were not easy. Having had our main residence in western Massachusetts, we were unprepared for the cost of housing in the Boston area. We considered areas close to the city that had reasonably good school systems, but we hesitated. Marlene, who had taught in Boston for over ten years, was fearful about raising black children, especially black boys, in the city. She had heard too many stories from her African American college students about being followed in stores or questioned or arrested in a sweep of their neighborhood after a violent incident. And we both knew that too many young black boys had been gunned down in the street.

So we began to look for a home in the suburbs. The communities closest to Boston were too expensive, and we knew also that we had to be thinking about relatively equal commuting time to work for both of us. In the final analysis, we made our choice based on finding a house we really liked for a price we could afford. Our choice turned out fine for our sons, but not because we knew what we were doing. We were just lucky.

If we had known then what we know now, we would have made a different choice. But we didn't. We did a cursory check of the community and the schools. We knew the community was primarily blue collar, working class with an influx of younger people who were buying homes in new developments springing up around town. The population wasn't particularly diverse but that was true of the other communities in the area. The number of high school students who graduated and the percentage of those students who went on to college were reasonably high, so we felt comfortable that the schools would be okay. What we didn't understand at this point in our adoption journey was that these characteristics were not "okay" for children of color and that there were also community factors underlying some of the statistics—for example, we didn't realize how few professional people lived in the community.

The newer members of the community, while considerably more affluent than the established residents, primarily comprised people who were working in the trades (builders, painters, electricians, plumbers) or small business owners. Few people in town held graduate degrees. When our children were older and getting ready to go to school, we realized that we didn't want them to attend a school where children didn't have high aspirations. And every black friend we had told us the same. Our neighbors down the street whose daughter and son were teenagers when we moved in, once told Fern that they were hopeful that their daughter would start college so she could meet a young man to marry! And they expected that their son would join his father's house painting business when he graduated from high school. These people became good friends, and their daughter was one of our first babysitters. But we wanted our children to be in a community with at least a solid core of people who had higher aspirations for their children and where gender roles were less traditional.

As we learned about being a multiracial family and parents of children of color, we came to see that U.S. culture doesn't have high expectations for African American children and that far too many people see high accomplishment by blacks outside of sports and entertainment as exceptional and surprising. It is imperative, therefore, that parents of these children set high expectations and that children meet and interact with others who share those expectations. African American parents know this. That is why they so fiercely push their children to succeed. They know that the culture won't push them; in fact, just the opposite. Media circulate images daily of youth of color that create a picture of gang violence, drug use, and teenage pregnancies. When successful African Americans are pictured, they are most often athletes or entertainers. That is one of the reasons why the election of Barak Obama was so important in communities of color. Children of color now had a role model in evidence *every day*; they could aspire to be or do anything, even President of the United States.

After living in our community for a few years, we began to look more closely at the colleges that students who graduated from the high school chose to attend. Most went to local state colleges or community colleges. A few attended the state university. Virtually none went to Ivy League schools and very few to other private colleges. Both of us are products of state universities, so the issue was not that we wanted our children to attend Ivy League or private schools. But we did want them to believe that they could aspire to attend them and to believe that high aspirations were something to value.

Our neighborhood proved to be a wonderful place for our children when they were young. We were only the third family on the street when we moved in. Over the next two years, other houses were built and, purely by chance, our street became multicultural, with an extended Chinese family living across from us, an Egyptian family next to them, and a mixed-race (African American/white) family and their children a few houses down. Everyone on the street had young children and the kids grew up playing in the street and going in and out of each others' homes as if they were theirs. People accepted our family. The boys attended a racially and socioeconomically mixed day care center when they were young and later attended a local

Montessori school that had some diversity. Although they didn't go to school with the other children in the neighborhood, they played with them after school and in the local soccer league on weekends. From the boys' perspective, it was an idyllic place to grow up.

And in many ways, it was. It was also a place that taught us about why race matters. Not because we encountered overt racism in the community, or, for that matter, more subtle forms of personal racism. We felt always that we and our children were accepted members of the neighborhood and the larger community. Marlene was even persuaded to coach one of the local soccer teams, even though she had never played soccer. But living in a white, working-class community with average schools taught us to be aware of more insidious ways that racism rears its ugly head, ways that are unknown to most whites.

Our experience choosing where we would live provides two key lessons. First, be sure that you dig beneath the surface when you do research on possible communities. It's not enough to know the racial composition of the community; you also need to know whether neighborhoods are racially and economically mixed. It's not enough to know the high school graduation rate; you also want to know the percentage of graduates who go on to college and what schools they attend. Second, try to envision your lives at various stages as your children get older. Our community was comfortable for our family when the boys were little, but its comfort level would have likely decreased when the little boys became teenagers.

But we're getting ahead of ourselves here. Let's return to the topic of decisions about adoption.

Adoption options—*"Who will be my child?"*

We moved into our new home in August and Marlene quickly finished the remaining requirements for her adoption application. Because Marlene planned to step down from her administrative position and return to the faculty full-time after our baby arrived, we tried to time the arrival of a baby so that she would be able to take maternity leave in the winter or spring and return to teaching in the fall. We released Marlene's home study in November and by early December we were told that a baby boy was available for adoption. We eagerly said we were interested and would like to look at the baby's file. We were so excited about this baby and so certain he would be right for us that we named him even before we "met" him through a photograph. Our first clue that something was off about this placement was when our social worker called and asked us to come to her office to discuss the baby's placement file. Carol, who was usually enthusiastic and forthcoming, would give us no information about the baby on the phone. She said she would share everything with us when we met with her. Carol was unusually quiet when we arrived at her office. After we were seated, she placed the file on a coffee table in front of her and took out a photograph. She held the photo for a moment and then quietly said we needed to know some things about the baby before we saw the photo. We waited expectantly, eager to see the photo and yet increasingly aware that something was amiss. "Our baby" had been born prematurely, she said. "How prematurely?" we asked. She said he was born at 24 weeks (that's less than six months) and then passed us the photo. As we looked at this tiny baby boy whose eyes were tightly closed, tears came to our eyes. We could barely hear Carol say that he most likely would be blind and would have severe developmental problems, giving him a poor prognosis for his physical and mental development.

What was happening to us at that moment wasn't supposed to happen in the adoption process. We had been very clear in our application that we didn't care about the sex of our child, the race of our child, the background of our child—but we did care about our child's developmental prospects for cognitive growth. And as two working professionals, we knew that we would be unable to give a child with disabilities the constant care and attention he or she would need. We understood that nothing in life is certain. A healthy baby might have an accident or develop an illness, or be diagnosed within a year or two with autism or another disability. Every parent must face the possibility that something might happen that would change a child's physical and/or mental capabilities. But adoption lets prospective parents accept or reject a referral, and even before that, specify factors of importance to them. We couldn't say yes to this baby.

Writing about our decision now sounds cold and calculating. At the time, it was heartbreaking. We knew that we could not assume responsibility for this child, but we also knew that if we turned down this referral, he was not likely to find another family willing to adopt him. The guilt and sadness were overpowering. We mourned as we assume parents mourn when a pregnancy ends in miscarriage. Looking back, we made the right decision for us. In the moment, however, we agonized over our decision, second guessing ourselves, convinced there would never be a child for us.

We share this story not as a cautionary tale about adoption, but in order to point out how important it is that prospective parents be clear with themselves and with their adoption agency about what kind of child they feel capable of caring for. Adoption is a commitment for life. Adoptive parents have taken a vow to love, cherish, and care for the child they adopt, so they need to be certain that they are willing to deal with whatever issues arise.

A child's race is not a disability. In fact, race, as we discuss in the next section of this chapter, is an artificial category system that was created to justify the economic and social class system that developed several centuries ago in the U.S. We believe that raising a child of another race is a privilege that gives parents the opportunity to learn with their child the richness inherent in difference. Choosing to raise a child of another race, however, is not a choice to be made lightly. Creating a family across racial differences takes work. Prospective parents need to:

- be open to learning about the role of race in culture

- be willing to teach their child about his or her racial heritage and to be proud of that heritage

- redefine themselves as members of a multiracial family

- understand that they will never experience the meaning of race in the way their child will.

Doing those things is a major lifetime commitment.

Race in U.S. society—*Race matters*

The role of race in American society is complex because of both its role in the history of the U.S. and its continuing role in economic and social class disparities. Despite the current political discourse that we are in a post-racial society, race continues to matter. In fact, a recent survey of Americans found that prejudice against blacks increased during President Barack Obama's first term in office from 2008–2012, with 51 percent of non-Hispanic whites surveyed expressing explicit racist attitudes toward blacks (up from 48% in 2008) and 56 percent expressing implicit racist attitudes toward blacks (up from 49%) (Agiesta and Ross 2012). There are two areas in which race matters to everyone, but especially affects people of color: *types of racism*, which include interpersonal racism, institutional racism, and internalized racism, and *racially-linked cultures*. White parents of black children need to become familiar with and understand these ongoing consequences of race. In the next section, we briefly introduce these concepts. We'll return to them throughout the remainder of the book.

That race matters, however, doesn't mean that race is "real," at least not in the sense that most people understand "real." Race is not a biological truism. In fact, there is scant biological evidence that supports the concept of race. Scientists now believe that all humans descended from the same ancestors in Africa; over thousands of years, people migrated to different parts of the world and adapted physiologically to those new environments (Roach 2008). After years of studying biological racial differences, scientists have discovered greater biological variation within each race than between them, which suggests that race is a category system based on something other than biological differences. In fact, our simplistic concept of race is socially constructed; it is a category system devised to explain and, in some instances, justify economic and social differences among different groups. In 1998, the American Anthropological Association issued a statement on race, saying that scholars today take the position that "race as it is understood in the United States was a social mechanism invented during the 18th century to refer to those populations brought together in colonial America: the English and other European settlers, the conquered Indian peoples, and those peoples of Africa brought in to provide slave labor." The existence of the slave trade demanded a means by which those who traded and those who owned slaves could justify the inhumane treatment of other human beings. Doing so demanded the creation of a category system that defined blacks as subhuman. Thus, racial categories were born. Hitler employed the same technique in defining the Aryan race as superior to Jews, gypsies, homosexuals, and others. There is no Aryan race. As a social construction, however, it served to justify the death camps to the German people.

Scientists do study small but important population differences that are race-based. For example, there appears to be a greater susceptibility to sickle-cell anemia in sub-Saharan descended populations, a finding that parents of black children should know. In Chapter 3, we discuss hair and skin concerns that many black people share and that most whites don't know about. The most significant effects of race, however, are the result of the social construction of race and racial difference rather than biological differences.

Types of racism

That race is socially constructed, however, doesn't negate its substantive and real consequences. White parents of black children must develop racial literacy, becoming knowledgeable about the history of racism and the ways it manifests itself in contemporary society. In this section, we provide a brief overview of the types of racism. Our overview barely scratches the surface of the subject. We encourage you to read more deeply about racism and we list some resources at the end of the chapter.

Racism ranges from the overt to the subtle and includes actions as disparate as the intentional racial slur to the practice of "redlining" in which banks charge higher interest rates for mortgages in communities of color. Racism is generally divided into three categories: interpersonal, institutional, and internalized.

INTERPERSONAL RACISM

Interpersonal racism refers to the mistreatment, verbally or physically, of one person by another person because of the other's race or ethnicity. The U.S. has a long history of racial violence, beginning with slavery and continuing through the 1900s with the widespread lynching of blacks in the South; race riots in numerous parts of the country, for example, in East St. Louis in 1917, Atlanta in 1906, and Omaha and Chicago in 1919; and numerous other forms of violence. In 1921, the white citizens of Tulsa, Oklahoma burned and looted homes and businesses in the black section of north Tulsa; estimates of the number of blacks who were killed exceed 100, making it the worst race riot in U.S. history. Although racial violence against blacks continues today (witness the February 2012 shooting death in Florida of Trayvon Martin, a young black man, by George Zimmerman, a white Hispanic, and the two white men who killed five blacks in Tulsa in April of the same year), the physical mistreatment of blacks by whites has decreased substantially. Today, blacks are more likely to encounter violence through black-on-black crime than through racial violence perpetrated by whites (Harrell 2007). Black-on-black violence in urban areas is a reality of life for many black youth. The history of racial violence directed at blacks, the racial riots of the 1960s in Watts, Newark, Detroit, and other cities in which blacks looted and set fire to businesses in black neighborhoods, and the growth of intra-racial crime point to the complexity of race and to the intersection of race and poverty.

Although the incidence of physical abuse based on interpersonal racism has lessened, verbal racism directed at blacks continues, even in a time of what some call "political correctness" when people are allegedly much more careful about what they say. In July 2012, a Boston Red Sox player, Carl Crawford, was called "Monday" as he walked onto the field by a person sitting in the stands. "Monday," a derogatory term for blacks, refers to the fact that Monday is the least liked day of the week, and is used as a euphemism for "nigger." This incident of verbal abuse is especially telling since the person in the stands turned out to be a white police officer, an individual charged with protecting all citizens.

Verbal racism isn't always intentional. Often, negative attitudes toward and beliefs about racial groups based on stereotypes lead to racist comments that were unintentional. We remember when a grade school teacher told us that one of our sons, who was struggling in school at the time, was "lazy." In fact, we knew he was working very hard, but the teacher's immediate response was to label our son with the racial stereotype of blacks as lazy. Much later we discovered he was having auditory processing problems related to hearing loss he experienced as a baby from repeated ear infections and ear tubes. Blacks, unfortunately, are accustomed to hearing such comments and dealing with them because *racial stereotypes* are now deeply embedded in our culture. Whether it's the circulation of negative and/or restrictive images of blacks by mainstream media, a teacher's statement that a B grade is good enough for a black child, a manager's call to security to follow black teens who are shopping in the store, or a police officer's decision to pull over a young black man driving on the highway (known among African Americans as a DWB—"driving while black"), negative stereotypes and profiling of blacks remain pervasive and harmful. White parents of black children need to become aware of these stereotypes and vigilant in identifying them, both in themselves and others.

INSTITUTIONAL RACISM

Institutional racism occurs when societal institutions (political, economic, or social) provide more advantages or resources to people of one race than another. There are significant and continuing disparities between whites and blacks in the U.S. that are the result of the long history of discrimination against blacks. White household incomes are two-thirds higher than black household incomes; white adults are more likely to have college degrees and own their own homes and less likely to live in poverty (Census report 2006). Blacks have less access to mental health care treatment (McGuire and Miranda 2008) and birth control (Cohen 2008), they are less likely to receive lifesaving treatment after suffering a stroke, and they are more likely to be obese and have untreated hypertension and heart disease (Peterson and Yancy 2009). These differences are largely the result of institutional racism that is the legacy of slavery and discrimination. That legacy directly affects the quality of life for African Americans.

For example, slavery made it difficult for blacks to create and maintain traditional families and also profoundly affected gender role identity. Black men first born into slavery and later freed only to face chronic unemployment or underemployment because of racism never had the opportunity to enact the white male gender role of family breadwinner. Black women, whether slave or free, have always had to work to support their families, a reality at odds with the historical white female gender role of wife who needs to be taken care of by her husband (which is also a myth for working-class white families). The legacy of slavery can also be seen in the economic situation of blacks in the U.S. Income disparities between whites and blacks can, in large part, be traced to the post World War II housing boom, when scores of middle-class whites purchased homes on easy credit and often with favorable government incentives. Blacks, however, didn't have equal access to credit because banks discriminated against them—and still do (Rothstein 2012). Over time, home ownership creates wealth. Whites who owned their own homes could live in good neighborhoods and send their children to good schools. They had the money to finance a college education for their children or to pay for college outright, which was then much more affordable. Their children then had access to better paying jobs, thus creating a self-perpetuating cycle of upward mobility and wealth accumulation. Professor Thomas Shapiro, author of *The Hidden Cost of Being African American* (2005), says that the increasing gap in wealth between whites and blacks "is not just a story of merit and achievement, it's also a story of the historical legacy of race in the United States" (as quoted in Census report 2006).

INTERNALIZED RACISM

Internalized racism occurs when individuals begin to believe prejudiced ideas about themselves or others who share their race or ethnicity. Internalized racism "gives rise to patterns of thinking, feeling and behaving that result in discriminating, minimizing, criticizing, finding fault, invalidating, and hating oneself while simultaneously valuing the dominant culture" (Lipsky 1987). Perhaps the best known example of internalized racism was seen in the studies done by Kenneth and Mamie Clark in the 1940s (Ahuja 2009). The Clarks, who were African

American sociologists, showed black children two dolls, one white and one black, and asked the children questions about them. The majority said that the white doll was nicer than the black doll and they would rather play with the white doll. Further, 44 percent of the children said that the white doll looked more like them than the black doll did.

The good news is that a 2009 replication of the original study suggests that the attitudes of black children about black dolls (and by implication, about themselves) have improved (Ahuja 2009). The ABC television show, "Good Morning America," recreated the Clark's experiment and found that 88 percent of the children identified with the black doll, 42 percent wanted to play with the black doll (only 32 percent preferred to play with the white doll and the remaining 26 percent had no preference), and the majority said that either the black doll was nicer or there was no difference between the black and white dolls. The bad news is that all these years later, signs of internalized racism still appeared. When asked which doll was more beautiful, 47 percent of the girls identified the white doll. And if we look more closely at the children's responses, we see further signs of internalized racism. For example, one child said the white doll was nicer because the black doll "talks back and don't follow directions" and another said the black doll was ugly because "sometimes this one has its feet like a monkey."

Racially-linked cultures

The second area in which race matters is associated with the development of *racially-linked cultures*. For example, a unique set of cultural characteristics have been passed down by generations of African Americans, including language, art, music, religious practice, literature, and modes of being and behaving. Over the long stretch of time since the beginning of slavery, those characteristics have blended African ways of understanding and being with the experience of being black in the United States.

We don't mean to suggest that African American culture and mainstream American culture are entirely separate entities. From music to fashion to hairstyles, black Americans have helped to shape the cultural lives of all Americans and the perception by other cultures of what is uniquely American. For example, many musicians throughout the world recognize jazz, which is an artifact of African American culture, as the quintessential American musical form. We will discuss African American culture in greater depth in later chapters, but we want to emphasize here the importance of introducing African American children to the reality of that culture.

Other groups, for example Chinese Americans, also have a heritage of racially-linked culture. In this case, the influence of Confucianism is responsible over the long term for values stressing obedience, respect for parents and elders, measured speech, and humility rather than boastfulness. Ethnic cultures also come into play for children of Hispanic background. The term "Hispanic" comprises numerous diverse cultures throughout the western hemisphere, such as Puerto Rican, Mexican, Cuban, Chilean, that differ in their family patterns and values, food preferences, dialects and accents, political history, etc. Adopted children need to learn about the specific cultures of their birth. Older adopted children will have internalized many values and practices of their birth cultures. And they (and their parents) also need to be aware of the stereotypes about those cultures that are prevalent in society, for example, that Asians are good at math or that Hispanics are lazy.

Most whites are unaware of how racism works and how race, ethnicity, and culture are linked. This is primarily because of what Peggy McIntosh (1992) calls *white privilege*. McIntosh says that whites carry "an invisible package of unearned assets." These assets or privileges include, for example, being in the company of people who are of the same race whenever they choose, turning on the television or going to the movies and seeing members of their race, finding a hairdresser who knows how to cut their hair, buying flesh colored bandages that match their skin, doing well without being called a credit to their race, or, conversely, not doing well and having that lack of success be attributed to their race. Perhaps the most significant privilege whites (or anyone who is a member of a majority culture that holds power) have is the ability to know nothing about the experiences and cultures of people who are not like them. White privilege means that being white is the norm against which everyone who is not white is measured. And even more powerfully, it means that when whites are in the company of other whites, they do not have to think about race at all. That is one reason why whites are often perplexed when they are asked to talk about being white. *White* is rarely seen by whites as a racial category.

Whites who adopt African American children must be prepared to unpack what McIntosh (1992) calls their "knapsack of privileges" and to open themselves to learning about and understanding the experiences of blacks. Some of that will come naturally through the experience of being a member of a mixed-race family. When we adopted our first child, we thought we understood the concept of privilege. Along with many feminists and academics, we had read and shared with our students McIntosh's work. As women, we had experienced the consequences of male privilege, but white privilege was a theoretical concept, an abstraction. We understood theoretically that as a white person we had privileges that black people didn't have—we could buy a house in any neighborhood (assuming we had sufficient money); we could walk the streets of our town without having someone call the police; we could drive without getting pulled over simply because we looked suspicious; we could shop without being followed by security guards; we could count on not being noticed in most places solely because we were white. That is, we could do these things before we became the parents of black children.

Parenting a black child taught us how little we knew about white privilege. When we were out with our son, strangers (white and black) would come up to us and almost tearfully tell us what wonderful people we were and how blessed our son was because we had adopted him. Would they have said the same if we were two black women with a white baby? We were doubtful. We also learned about not having privilege. As a tenured college professor with a Ph.D. and two master's degrees, Marlene experienced the world at the top of an intellectual and social class hierarchy (earned, not inherited). She tumbled quickly to the bottom of that hierarchy the day that she took our son to the local Social Security office to apply for his Social Security card. When her name was called, she—a white woman in jeans carrying a black baby—approached the desk. The clerk assumed she was there to pick up her monthly welfare check. Marlene was so shocked she couldn't speak.

It is not that having black children erased all of our white privileges. We still had many—and these spilled over and protected our children, especially when they were young. But white privilege became viscerally real rather than theoretical the day that we stopped to look at a beach house on Cape Cod with our two black children in tow, the older, now two years old, and the younger, an infant. The owner assured us that the house was available for rent that summer. We told her that we had a few other houses to look at and that we would call her the next morning if we still wanted the house. Marlene called early in the morning to say we were interested, but the woman said that the house was no longer available. Marlene got off the phone convinced that she would not rent to us because the children were black. The owner proved Marlene wrong a few hours later when she called back to say that she had convinced the people who had rented the house to change their rental dates because she thought our boys were adorable and would love staying in her house. The damage was done, however, because the moment she told Marlene that the house was no longer available to rent,

Marlene understood the horror of believing that everything that happens to you might be because of your skin color. We both understood how that belief would constantly haunt us and would distort our understanding of events in our lives and our children's lives (we discuss racial vigilance in Chapter 5 as it relates to what happens in school). Why didn't he get a solo in the band concert? Why was he left out of the team photograph? We even questioned the good things that happened, thinking that the boys sometimes received good grades or accolades simply because they were black and other people either had low expectations for them or were afraid to judge them fairly for fear of being called racist or having us in their faces.

Most whites also know very little about African American culture and experience because whites and blacks generally live in different neighborhoods and travel in different friendship circles. Whites often say they have African American friends, but they usually mean that they have colleagues at work or one or two friends from school. Rarely do blacks and whites have the kinds of friendships in which they talk about and experience together the intimate details of their lives outside of public contexts or in the kind of intimacy of similarity that makes "race talk" an unselfconscious occurrence. There are many reasons for the continued separation of blacks and whites. Dr. Marsha Houston, an African American woman who is a good friend of ours, has studied communication between black and white women, and she terms their conversations "difficult dialogues" (2012, first published in 1994). She says that white women and black women have different expectations about conversation and those different expectations lead them to assess the talk of the other negatively. White women believe that black women don't speak with proper grammar, diction, and decorum, and black women believe that white women talk around issues, avoiding conflict and not saying what they mean. The lack of understanding leads white women to assume that black women are inferior and black women to assume that white women are untrustworthy, making conversations between them "difficult dialogues." Although these may strike some as stark characterizations, they point to the ways in which communication between white people and black people can be fraught because of assumptions and conflicts in how meanings are understood based on what is said and how it is said.

There are many areas of cultural differences between African Americans and whites, and we will discuss those differences throughout the book. We don't expect that most white Americans who are considering the possibility of adopting an African American child are familiar with all of these differences. We weren't when we adopted our sons—and we're quite sure there are many differences we still don't know. What you know, however, as you begin your adoption journey is not as important as your understanding that race still matters and you need to be open to learning about why and how it matters. There are also, of course, many cultural similarities between whites and blacks, and one of those is the desire to love and nurture their children and to do as much as possible to ensure their children will grow up to be healthy and happy adults. Our goal in describing some of the challenges in cross-racial adoption is not to discourage or frighten a prospective adoptive parent, but to give a realistic idea of some of the issues you will face if you decide to adopt a child of another race and the kind of work you will need to do to negotiate life in a multiracial family. We believe that the rewards of taking on these issues are enormous. In addition to creating a loving family, you will increase your understanding of both what it means to be different in our culture and the many dimensions of our shared humanity. In Chapter 3, we'll discuss some strategies to help your child develop a healthy racial identity. Next, however, we help you think about how to talk about race and adoption with your family and friends.

Things to consider

- *Race matters.* Examine your own preconceptions and prejudices, and whether you can commit to loving a child of color unconditionally.

- *Where you live matters.* What does your community offer your child—a diverse population? Good schools? High community aspirations for young people? Are you willing to move to ensure that your child grows up in a community that is welcoming?

- *Your flexibility and openness to change matter.* Adopting a child of color will change your life forever. You will no longer be able to assume your identity as a white person and the privileges that you've enjoyed because of that identity. Are you willing to deal with those changes?

References

Agiesta, J. and Ross, S. (2012) "Poll finds majority hold racist views." *The Boston Globe*, 27 October, p. A4. Available at www.bostonglobe.com/news/nation/2012/10/27/poll-majority-harbor-prejudice-against-blacks/5Tj42nmGdF8e4iF0FQ0aNK/story.html, accessed on 7 February 2013.

Ahuja, G. (2009) "What a doll tells us about race." 31 March. Available at abcnews.go.com/GMA/story?id=7213714&page=1, accessed on 14 March 2013.

American Anthropological Association (1998) *American Anthropological Association Statement on Race.* 17 May. Available at www.aaanet.org/stmts/racepp.htm, accessed on 7 February 2013.

"Census report: Broad racial disparities persist." (2006) NBCNEWS.com. 14 November. Available at www.msnbc.msn.com/id/15704759#.UCPNHGGP98E, accessed on 7 February 2013.

Cohen, S.A. (2008) "Abortion and women of color: The bigger picture." *Guttmacher Policy Review 11*, 3. Available at www.guttmacher.org/pubs/gpr/11/3/gpr110302.html, accessed on 18 October 2012.

Gerson, M. (2012) "The ignored plight of black males." *The Washington Post*, 14 December, p. A29.

Harrell, E. (2007) *Black Victims of Violent Crime.* Washington, D.C.: Bureau of Justice Statistics. Available at bjs.gov/content/pub/pdf/bvvc.pdf, accessed on 14 March 2013.

Herbert, B. (2010) "Too long ignored." *New York Times*, 21 August, p.19.

Hooda, S. (2012) "Unemployment rates highest amongst Blacks and Latinos." Huffington Post, 10 September. Available at www.huffingtonpost.com/2012/09/10/unemployment-rates-highest-amongst-black-and-latinos_n_1871453.html, accessed 19 March 2013.

Houston, M. (2012/original 1994) "When Black Women Talk with White Women: Why the Dialogues Are Difficult." In A. Gonzalez, M. Houston, and V. Chen (eds) *Our Voices: Essays in Culture, Ethnicity, and Communication*, 5th ed. New York: Oxford University Press.

Lipsky, S. (1987) *Internalized Racism*. Seattle, WA: Rational Island Publishers. Available at www.rc.org/publications/journals/black_reemergence/br2/br2_5_sl.html, accessed on 19 March 2013.

McGuire, T.G. and Miranda, J. (2008) "New evidence regarding racial and ethnic disparities in mental health: Policy implications." *Health Affairs 27*, 2, 393–403.

McIntosh, P. (1992) "White Privilege and Male Privilege." In A.L. Andersen and P.H. Collins (eds) *Race, Class and Gender*. Belmont, CA: Wadsworth.

NABSW (1972) "Position statement on trans-racial adoption." September. Available at pages.uoregon.edu/adoption/archive/NabswTRA.htm, accessed on 17 March 2013.

NABSW (2003) "Preserving families of African ancestry." 10 January. Available at www.nabsw.org/mserver/PreservingFamilies.aspx, accessed on 17 March 2013.

Peterson, E. and Yancy, C.W. (2009) "Eliminating racial and ethnic disparities in cardiac care." *New England Journal of Medicine 360*, 12, 1172–1174.

Roach, J. (2008) "Massive genetic study supports 'Out of Africa' Theory." *National Geographic News*, 21 February. Available at news.nationalgeographic.com/news/2008/02/080221-human-genetics.html, accessed on 14 March 2013.

Rothstein, R. (2012) "A comment on Bank of America/Countrywide's discriminatory mortgage lending and its implications for racial segregation." *Economic Policy Institute Briefing Paper #335*, January 23. Available at www.epi.org/publication/bp335-boa-countrywide-discriminatory-lending, accessed on 7 February 2013.

Shapiro, T.M. (2005) *The Hidden Cost of Being African American: How Wealth Perpetuates Inequality*. New York: Oxford University Press.

The Adoption Foundation (2011) "Gender preference." Available at www.adoption.com, accessed on 7 February 2013.

West, C. (1993) *Race Matters*. Boston, MA: Beacon Press.

Resources

http://colorlines.com.

This daily news site, produced by the Applied Research Center, a national racial justice think tank, provides up-to-the-minute investigative reports and news analyses about racism in the U.S.

Cracking the Codes: The System of Racial Inequity (DVD) (2012) World Trust
Organization.
This film, directed by Shakti Butler, provides a compelling and provocative account
of the causes and consequences of systemic inequity in the U.S. Check your local
library for copies of the DVD. For information about the DVD, see the following
website, available at *http://world-trust.org/cracking-the-codes-understanding-the-system-
of-inequity.*

Henry, M.J. and Pollack, D. (2009) *Adoption in the United States: A Reference for
Families, Professionals, and Students*. Chicago, IL: Lyceum Books.
This volume provides a detailed overview of research related to a range of adoption
issues, including legal, financial, and medical issues, agency versus private adoptions,
domestic versus international adoptions, and diverse family configurations.

Lazarre, J. (1999) *Beyond the Whiteness of Whiteness*. Durham, NC: Duke University
Press.
Lazarre's memoir of a white mother of black sons poignantly explores the pervasiveness
of racism in American society.

Massey, D. and Denton, N. (1993) *American Apartheid: Segregation and the Making
of the Underclass*. Cambridge, MA: Harvard University Press.
Massey and Denton explore de facto residential segregation and its consequences in
the U.S.

Parks, G.S. and Hughey, M.W. (eds) (2011) *12 Angry Men: True Stories of Being a
Black Man in America Today*. New York: The New Press.
This volume explores African American men's experiences with racial profiling.

CHAPTER 2

Talking about Race and Adoption—

"You're Doing What?!"

The first time a white person mentions that he or she is considering adopting a child of another race—especially a black child—comments come from every possible direction. Some responses are minimal and unelaborated: "Oh cool" "Oh wow!" "That should be interesting" or simply "Ooohh." Some express surprise but acceptance, even enthusiasm. Others express surprise and skepticism. Predicting who will respond in what way proves to be less than perfect. We were surprised, for instance, when Marlene's parents did not respond well to the news that we were planning to adopt an African American baby. These were liberal people with positive racial views. Yet, when faced with the idea of their grandchild being black, they hesitated and seemed to think it was their role to advise against it. Their response would change over time, but we'll get to that a little later.

Talking with black friends and acquaintances about adopting across race often produces even more tension and hand-wringing for whites than talking about it with white friends and acquaintances. It's good to start these conversations well before you make a final decision. When we were considering adopting a black child in the late 1980s, we worried about how black friends would respond to us based on the position of the National Association of Black Social Workers that what we were contemplating was a form of racial genocide. Would they sympathize with that position? Should we talk about it in the abstract with them before broaching the subject that WE are considering INTERRACIAL ADOPTION? Yes, *we*. We found that candor worked best for these discussions—not only when adoption was still in the future but also later as African Americans came into our lives, either through community or professional contacts. As a rule, the more you can learn about how racism and racial thinking works in our society, the better prepared you will be for the twists, turns, and topics of conversation. If a black friend or acquaintance is skeptical about the decision you are contemplating, ending the conversation or running away is a lost opportunity. It's important to listen, to probe, and to learn as much as possible about the range of ideas and experiences that a non-black person needs to be exposed to.

Listening, probing, and learning will take on new directions as you think through the adoption process, from the start to where you are at the moment. In the context of interracial adoption, we heard things about race and ethnicity that we never heard before—not because they were not said but because we were not tuned to listen in a particular way. We also interpreted differently with this new perspective. It's a little like the proverbial cat ears heading in every direction where there are elements of race or ethnicity to be heard or seen.

In this chapter, we cover four major issues that arise when people talk about race and adoption with others. Although not a comprehensive list, these four topics are certain to be significant:

- Deciding what information about your child to share with others

- Responding to racist and hurtful comments

- Calculating how to navigate situations where you are suspicious that subtle (or not so subtle) racism is operating in response to your child, and

- Dealing with well-meaning people who want to cast you as a savior because you are a white person who intends to or already has adopted a non-white child.

Sharing information about my child's background—*"Do tell us everything!"*

During our home study process, a social worker wisely advised us that adopted children should never hear something important about their background that their adopted parents had not told them. It doesn't matter, she said, if the person is a family member, close friend, or teacher. The point is that your child should not be surprised or taken off guard by information that she or he has not heard from you, the parent. The advice seemed reasonable at the time, but we didn't know how important it would be or how many times we would be tested—by close friends, relatives, acquaintances, and total strangers. Although usually well meaning, questions about the circumstances of our children's background came frequently and with the expectation that we would respond with the information requested. We thought some of the questions were insensitive, while others were completely understandable, even if we were not going to answer them. The range of questions was wide but also predictable at some level. These were questions that had been on our minds too. "Was your son's birth mother a teenager?" "Did the birth father abandon the mother?" "Did the birth mother drink or take drugs when she was pregnant?" "How dark is his skin?" These and many other questions reminded us that decisions about what to tell to whom and when to tell them need careful thought.

Time for careful thought is not always possible though, especially when the person asking the question is standing next to you and expecting a reply. The first time someone asks about the background of your child, your impulse is likely to want to share what you know. You're excited, as any prospective parent would be, to talk about the child who will soon be joining your family. You're eager, as any parent is, to talk about your child with others. To keep our heads from spinning about exactly what we might want to tell to whom and what we had already told person x or y, we tried to keep the social worker's advice front and center in our minds.

As a rule, we decided that we would not disclose specific information about our children's backgrounds beyond what was visible to anyone, even family members and close friends, unless there was a good reason or circumstances made it important to do so. For example, we were visiting Fern's sister and brother-in-law in Minnesota when we received the news that our younger son was available for adoption. We had to make a very quick decision and needed to talk through an issue related to the adoption. We shared the information with them, but asked them to keep it confidential. Knowing ahead of time how we were going to respond to questions from other people about our children's backgrounds allowed us to be prepared for the questions when they were asked. Other adoptive parents that we knew did not approach the issue in quite the same way. Some chose to share details of the birth parents with close friends, while others shared details only with others who had adopted or were planning to adopt. Our point here is that it is important for you to decide how you plan to respond before you get the questions. Whatever choice you make, you want to be consistent in your responses and ready for the consequences.

All prospective parents are eager to share news about possible placements and eventually about the placement that will result in a child becoming part of the family. It's important not to be isolated when you are deciding about what is feasible.

For example, it's important for most people (both couples and singles) to have a sounding board for juggling all of the possibilities for who the adopted child might be and whether you can handle those possibilities. Certainly we were eager to talk with friends, family members, and new-found connections in the adoption network about everything from health issues, to age of the child, to ethnic and race background.

The types of information and the completeness of information about an adopted child's birth origins vary considerably depending on where the child is from, what the placement situation is, and whether or not the adoption is open. If the adopted child is older, there will also be information about foster parents and, perhaps, experiences with one or both birth parents. In some situations, it is important to be as thorough as possible about reporting on background information, for example, with a pediatrician or in some cases (but not all) a school psychologist. But what about family and friends? In our experience, almost all questions from family and friends flowed from genuine interest and caring for our family. Yet, we often relied on the social worker's advice that urged caution. Until you have shared all the information you have about your child's background with your child, many things are better left private. For example, in response to the question, "What do you know about your child's birth parents?" you might decide that it's okay to reveal that one was African American and the other Latino/a. If you also add that the birth mother had already given birth to two other children, you risk your child learning that information from the person you've told rather than from you.

In general, by age 12, you should be sharing all the information that you have about your child's background with your child (Keefer and Schooler 2000). At that point, the issue is not one of your child potentially learning something about his or her background that you did not disclose but, rather, of your deciding what information is private and only your child's to share. For example, if your child is HIV-positive or you have information suggesting that there may be a genetic predisposition toward some disease, you will have to decide *with your child* who should know about this in addition to physicians. If your child learns information about his or her birth parents that is tragic or disturbing to the child, it's probably best to limit who knows this information to intimate friends and family members. Depending on the nature of the background information and the child, it may be important to participate with your child in counseling, but this will depend on how the child deals with the information. You will also need to decide—*again with your child*—if you would share this type of information with any other people. These are difficult decisions to make, and they should be treated with care. The most important point here is that decisions such as these should be anticipated so that you are not caught off guard when they arise. An excellent statement of the bottom line here is from Keefer and Schooler, who say, "Remember that the history belongs to the child, not to the adoptive parents" (Keefer and Schooler 2000, p.94).

Responding to racist and hurtful comments and behavior—*"How dark is your baby?"*

A woman sitting next to Fern one night at a professional dinner asked if she had children. She replied that she had a two-year-old adopted son. The woman then asked what country the child was from. Fern replied, "He's from the U.S. and is African American." The woman then asked, "Is he very dark?" The question was insensitive, but since the dinner had not progressed beyond the salad course, "no response" was not an option. So Fern simply said, "My son is African American, and that means it's likely that both Africans and whites are in his biological background."

In addition to questions about your child's skin color, you are likely to get questions about *why* you are thinking of or have already adopted a child of color. "Did you try to adopt a white child?" is a question directed to many whites who have decided or are open to adopting a child of another race. The underlying assumption is that a white person would first try to adopt a white child, with the implication that for some reason it just didn't work out. On the face of it, the question is not necessarily racist. The person asking could simply be mentally thinking through a process that would have resulted in a decision to adopt a child of another race. Alternatively, the person asking the question may be assuming that a non-white child is a last resort, and if the child is black, the potency of that assumption is enhanced. Along the path to adoption there might be a number of statements and questions that are racially laced to imply something negative about the child: "Are most black babies up for adoption from mothers who are addicted to crack?" "Did your child have fetal alcohol syndrome?" Even though it might be comforting to simply dismiss the person who made the comment or asked the question as ignorant, these are things that keep working their way through our minds. If we don't respond at all or provide a curt reply, we may wind up replaying this in our head.

So, how should you respond? We think that directness is usually best, but also that it may be necessary to do more than provide a simple answer to a question or a blunt reply to a comment. Replying to communication that seems to be racist can be an opportunity to raise the question or comment to a higher plane. For example, if asked whether you first tried to adopt a white child, you might reply that most adoptive parents are presented with a broad range of options to think about so that they can make informed decisions that feel comfortable and right for them. This moves the topic to a more informative level and may possibly provide new and useful information for the person who asked the question. If the person makes a comment or asks a question that reveals ignorance, stereotyping, or lack of information and you know how to correct it, this is an opportunity to do so. Some questions are ones that probe for information that you would not provide in any case, but you can still provide some type of answer that is informative. Suppose a person says that she has heard there is a higher risk that black babies will have learning disabilities. You could reply by simply saying that, "We're not sharing specific information about our child, but there is a lot of information and research being done now on the causes and symptoms associated with very specific types of learning disabilities." If your adopted child is older and in school, certain school personnel will need to know more about her or his background. A teacher or school counselor might ask about whether anyone in your child's birth family has been diagnosed with Attention Deficit Hyperactivity Disorder. The question is a legitimate one for them to ask. Following the question with a statement that suggests that there is a higher incidence of ADHD among black children, however, is not legitimate, and it would be important for you to point out that the research on ADHD does not indicate higher rates among black children (Centers for Disease Control and Prevention 2011). If you discover that your child does have ADHD (or any other learning disorder), talking with other parents whose children have ADHD may help you cope with the diagnosis and will reassure you that learning disabilities are present among children of varied backgrounds.

There are some patterns to the types of racist comments that come up when you are parenting a black child, and we'll say more about some of these in subsequent chapters, for example, the seemingly benign and not so benign comments encountered in the school context. In this chapter we focus on more general points and offer advice on how to manage your own responses and be helpful to your child in situations where racist comments have been made or something has happened involving race that is hurtful or has a negative impact.

White parents of children of color are in a unique zone when in the context of other whites who do not know that they are the parents of or are anticipating being the parents of a child of color. We have often heard racist and racially ignorant comments from people who did not know we had two black sons and therefore were not monitoring or editing what they said: comments that repeat stereotypes that blacks are naturally athletic or more oriented to art than science; comments that question why a specific black student was admitted to a particular college; comments that blacks enjoy special privileges and advantages in society. Often these comments made us boil, yet they also helped us understand what some people believe. In Chapter 1, we discussed "white privilege"—what McIntosh characterizes as "an invisible package of unearned assets." Hearing comments from those unaware of our situation as parents of black children demonstrated one aspect of white privilege: a white person can make comments about race to other whites that she or he would not make if people of color were present. There is a certain "in group" feel in these situations—even with relative strangers. In most cases, we have tried to be vigilant in responding, sometimes without even saying anything about our personal situation as parents. In other cases, we have let things go without comment. Sometimes it's a matter of choosing what battles to fight or deciding to what extent a response might harm a relationship with the other person when that relationship is important.

There are also many white people who think they "know" what it is like to be a person of color. These are people who deny that there is differential treatment depending on one's race or who are bold enough to assert that verifiable information is incorrect. Both of us have heard whites deny that discrimination in lending still exists or that there is any such thing in this day and age as DWB—"Driving while black" or SWB—"Shopping while black." Solid research documents that all three practices exist. The DWB risk especially concerns parents of young black men who will likely experience the impact of DWB soon after they are out on their own driving a car. They will likely be followed and/or stopped for no justifiable reason (Staples 2009). Both of our sons experienced this soon after they had their driver's licenses. One was followed on an interstate highway by a state trooper who would alternate moving parallel in the left lane to get a good look at who was driving and then falling back behind the car. The other son, who was with a Latino friend and had parked on a street near our home in the middle of the afternoon, was stopped by a white police officer and asked for his name and where he lived. When our son gave his address two streets away, the police officer instructed him to "Be on your way." Fortunately, neither young man was asked to get out of the car. Other young black men have not fared so well. DWB frequently is the subject of news reports. One graphic illustration is shown in a nine-minute investigative report broadcast on UPN9 television in Nassau county, New York in 2008 (Driving While Black). The segment shows a black male being stopped for no apparent reason by a white police officer, removed from his car, and interrogated about his reason for being in this particular location. The journalist then comments, "Unless they [the police] suspect criminal activity, they're not supposed to ask personal questions." When either of us tells other white people about such incidents, they often respond in a manner that suggests what happened is outrageous and *out of the ordinary*. A similar response often follows statements that a black girl or woman is more likely to be under surveillance in a store than a white woman. A black female colleague often told of being taught explicitly never to go into a store with a large purse, which would be pretty difficult in today's fashion craze of suitcase-sized purses! More importantly, this is not something that white women think about because it is one of those "white privileges." The pattern points to the continuation of racial profiling in which blacks are singled out as suspicious simply because they are black.

Fern recently had an experience with students who were analyzing an interview with two experts—one a white man and the other a black woman—who were talking about proposed legislation in Massachusetts to change the seat belt law from one where the police can only enforce the law if a driver is stopped for some other matter to one where the police can stop a person suspected of not wearing a seat belt. The white man was presenting a well-reasoned case for increasing the level of enforcement based on accident statistics and seat belts, and the black woman was arguing that the proposed legislation would give the police yet another reason to stop black drivers, especially males. The only student who sided with the black woman was the one black student in the class—a male—and it was only after he cited his own experience being stopped by police a number of times when he was not charged with doing anything illegal that the other students accepted the reasoning as valid. We can't know how the black student felt by having to explain his position, but Fern felt sadness and concern for how he was forced to reveal personal information that was possibly humiliating for him. It turned out to be a "teachable moment" about the ways in which race is both experienced and perceived differently. The situation vividly displayed how the taken-for-granted ideas of whites, in this case that the best argument is a well-reasoned and logically developed position with supporting research evidence, may trump the truth of minority experience *until* an actual person of color speaks up to explain a different perspective. Another recent example was reported in *The Boston Globe* Editorial & Opinion page. Kenny Wiley (2012), a 24-year-old Harvard Divinity School student, recounted his experience one night when he was running through Harvard Yard to try to catch a bus. As he ran past four strangers, one man yelled, "Bro, you running from the cops or something?" and a woman added, "What'd you steal this time?" Wiley's point in writing about this incident was "for us to stop pretending that racism is over." He was profiled, as are many blacks—both men and women.

When comments are made that seem racist, they can feel hurtful simply because they diminish our child or imply that she or he will not be on an equal footing with whites. The first name of one of our sons is the same as a famous basketball player. We named him after one of Fern's grandfathers and never connected his name with the basketball player. Yet many people asked if we named him after this basketball player. The hurt was that the comment suggested an expectation or aspiration for our son as well as the stereotype that black male role models should be athletes. When you hear something that is both racist and hurtful, it's important to be frank in responding. This shifts the racist comment, even if made innocently, back to the person who made it and, we hope, prompts reconsideration. In the case of the name associated with a basketball player, the response might be, "No, he was named after Fern's grandfather." Funny how no one would ask if a white girl named Anne was named after the actor Anne Hathaway or a white boy named Derek was named after the baseball player Derek Jeter.

Racist and hurtful comments also come from those close to us, both family members and friends. The discourse about racial preference in adoption abounds and comes from every possible direction. What might it mean when a friend or family member who is considering adoption tells you that they had hoped to adopt a Russian baby but will probably be adopting a Chinese baby because of availability, BUT NEVER MENTIONS THE OPTION OF ADOPTING A BLACK CHILD? A comment like this suggests an order of racial preference from white to Asian to black. One response is to simply say that there are also many black, Hispanic, and biracial children in the U.S. waiting to be placed in homes, rather than letting the comment stand without reply. You could also give examples of people other than yourselves who had many options available and decided that adopting a black child was their choice. The point here is not to make the person feel guilty or embarrassed for what was said but, rather, to be sure that the unstated assumption that a black child is not desirable is challenged, even if gently.

When white family members make comments that show disapproval or lack of enthusiasm for your plans to adopt a child of color, responding requires a good balance of candor and understanding. The bottom line, however, is that this is *your* choice about *your immediate family*. If a parent or sibling expresses concern or disapproval, one option is to say that the opinion is theirs, but you want your child to enjoy the love of grandparents, aunts and uncles, and hope that they will reconsider their position and what it implies about their future role in your family's life.

Is racism at work here?—*On guard!*

It still amazes us that we encounter so many examples of racially-linked words and actions that put us on guard. Some absolutely require a response, but—as mentioned earlier—decisions also have to be made about what battles to fight and when to grit your teeth and let certain things roll off your back.

Racial thinking—*the social ideas that shape the way that we learn to understand the world in racial terms*—is at the root of many types of comments and behavior. Racial thinking is inescapable but also changes over time (Spickard and Daniel 2004 offer one useful historical review). Evidence of racial thinking that is problematic but not necessarily laced with racism and prejudice will be more evident to whites who parent children of color than to those who do not. Glances and stares at white adults with dark-skinned or Asian-appearing children are commonplace, simply because the norm is for children to appear racially identical to their parents. Every white adoptive parent of a child of color adjusts to this and simply has to accept that their family will be noticed. Sometimes there will be explicit questions. It's common, for example, for young children (of any race) to notice and ask questions about a mis-match of a parent's and child's race. "You can't be his mommy," as Marlene was told by a child in preschool who seemed perplexed that her son was black and she was white. There are several possible responses to comments like this. A simple answer that, "There are many different kinds of families" might be enough. When children are a little older, it's fine to say that, "We adopted her and now we are a family."

Questions from adults that reveal racial thinking range from relatively benign questions, such as, "Did you adopt your child?" or "Where is your child from?" to more problematic questions such as, "Is she yours or adopted?" This last question also suggests an assumption that adoption creates a lesser family bond. Our response to that question would be, "She's adopted, which means she's our child." Biracial couples who have adopted children where one parent looks similar to the child's race but the other does not will experience different questions depending on the situation. Strangers will likely assume that a parent perceived to be the same race as the child is a biological parent. This perception may or may not be altered in the presence of the other parent who does not "racially match" the child. These questions and perceptions are not necessarily racist, but they always re-spark the feeling of being treated differently. The level of awareness of race simply increases dramatically when racial thinking shows up in concrete ways.

More difficult situations arise when the words or actions of others point to some type of racism—potential or actual. For example, a white parent of black children must be vigilant at all times, even more so than a black parent simply because whites need to learn the cues and clues of racism that are often missed because of both white privilege and lack of training and sensitivity to what situations and topics might include racial overtones. In a conversation about the possibility of a racial motive behind an administrative decision, one of Fern's black male faculty colleagues remarked to the (white) provost that there were many things that happened that he suspected were racist or racially motivated but that he also knew that he would not always be right. His point was that, as a black person, he needed to remain vigilant about racism (and racial thinking too) and to point out the possibility when he suspected it was present.

School is one site where vigilance is especially important (more will be said about this in Chapter 5). Many black friends warned us that we needed to be alert to teachers and other school personnel having lower expectations of our black sons than might be warranted. We encountered this several times when it was clear to us that a teacher's assessment of "doing well" (or well enough) fell short of what we thought our child was capable of. It's important for parents to question the teacher's expectations in this instance.

- "Why do you believe that she can't do 'A' level work?"

- "What skills does she lack to achieve a higher grade?"

- "What would she need to do to improve?"

It's possible that the teacher's assessment of your child's ability is correct. As professors, both of us have encountered students who believe that they deserve an "A" when they do not, a belief often based on the high grades they received in high school. Teachers often complain that many parents believe their children deserve higher grades than they receive, and they can get angry or defensive when parents question their assessments of their children. But parents of black children need to question those assessments to ensure that they are fair and not based on racial stereotypes. You can ask what the assessment is based on and even share your concerns about stereotyping in ways that are non-confrontational yet firm.

In addition to the possibility of facing lower expectations from teachers, a black child also runs the risk of being labeled "lazy" if the teacher thinks he or she is not working hard enough. We experienced this first-hand, as did several other parents of black children who we know. In situations like this, it's important to probe, to ask questions, and sometimes to challenge outright:

- "Why do you think he's lazy?"

- "What exactly has he done or not done?"

- "Could there be some reason why he isn't performing at the level that you think he should be at?"

- "Could you offer a more constructive approach to my son's situation than to call him lazy?"

For those who adopt children of Chinese background, this dynamic can work in the opposite direction, with the teacher's expectations over-reaching what is reasonable for the child. Asians are good at math, right? Asian kids are obedient and follow directions, right? These are stereotypes, and in some cases the specific child might fit the type but in other cases not.

The school context presents many challenges for all parents of children of color. We will address issues related to school and race in more detail in Chapter 5. Here we consider the ways in which school curriculum and teacher expectations linger as sources of *institutional racism*, which we talked about briefly in the previous chapter. Institutional racism occurs because of societal patterns rather than individual bias. Individuals often make decisions or act in ways that support these patterns. Such actions and decisions are made even by people who otherwise celebrate diversity and do not support prejudice. It's simply difficult to know the balance in a particular case of personal racism and the weight of tradition and social and institutional practices that devalue or discriminate against those who are not white. Children's books and school materials are definitely less likely today to exclude or demean blacks, Asians, and Hispanics than in the past, but issues still arise that demand a response from parents of children of color. If the only African American historical figures included in the school curriculum are Martin

Luther King, Jr. and Harriet Tubman, then it's likely that the only story of blacks in the U.S. that children will learn is one of a few milestones against racism. If books are available that include black, Asian, Hispanic, and Native American children but all or most of the authors are white, there's a problem in decision-making caused by institutional racism. Yes, white authors are more numerous, but that does not excuse the omission of authors of color. If book titles are limited and teaching units lack the full range of diversity, parents will need to assert themselves and gain the support of parents who are white and whose children are white. Many resources are available that cover diversity and children's literature; sorting through them takes time. Libraries in cities with diverse populations often house more children's books focused on diversity than will be found elsewhere. Certain awards, such as the American Library Association's Coretta Scott King Awards for outstanding books by African American authors and illustrators can provide appropriate book lists. The Database of Award-Winning Children's Literature (www.dawcl.com) provides a resource for searching books that meet multiple criteria, including the race of the characters, age of reader, genre, time period, and so forth. Part of the struggle against institutional racism is exposure to information that we were not taught and that most teachers were not taught.

We caution, however, that either suggesting or telling a teacher outright that she or he is racist or that the curriculum is in some way racist can be explosive. A constructive approach requires careful thought and preparation. If, for instance, you suspect that your child is being singled out by a teacher to speak for African Americans or Chinese Americans, you will need to contact the teacher and talk through the issue. The teacher may, in fact, be your ally, making it especially important not to alienate her or him. Perhaps the teacher's intention was to bring diverse viewpoints into a discussion without knowing that it would be inappropriate to single out a student—any student—to speak on behalf of a racial group.

A range of other types of comments and expectations about adopted children of color also arise in ways that need to be addressed. We have been asked countless times if our two sons are "brothers." In every case the question assumes that *brothers* = *blood brothers*. We always respond by saying that, "If you're asking if they had the same birth parents, 'no.' But *yes, they are brothers* and have been part of our family since they were infants." As our sons got older and their physical appearances clearly differed, we still got the same question about their being brothers, along with comments such as, "They look so much alike"—which they do not. Even more astonishing, several people also asked if our sons, who are nearly two years apart in age, are twins! What we seemed to be confronting was a lack of differentiation in how whites tend to perceive blacks—"all blacks look alike."

Other ethnic groups encounter similar stereotypes. Katrina Fryklund, one of Fern's students, interviewed college-aged adoptees from Latin American countries for her senior honors thesis project. One comment made by these young adults was that they frequently were in situations where strangers simply expected them to speak Spanish. This is particularly interesting in that many U.S.-born Hispanics of similar age do not speak Spanish either. An expectation that "Hispanic" and "brown skin" equals Spanish speaker seems to be at work here. Another example points to a similarity between African Americans and those of Latino/a background, where members of both groups are often assumed to be the beneficiaries of affirmative action and preferential treatment—translated to mean "unqualified" or "less qualified." A white friend recounted a personal story of this type of stereotyping. His son, who was adopted from Peru, was struggling academically during his first year of college at an institution where he met the academic requirements for his entering class. Our friend was comparing notes with an acquaintance about how their kids were faring in the college transition. The acquaintance's response to the news that the first year wasn't going smoothly was to ask if the college was too challenging academically and to wonder aloud if perhaps they admitted our friend's son in order to boost their "Hispanic numbers." Our friend's report is that he was careful to state that his son was qualified for this college but that there were other issues. In a situation like this one, other points could be made, for example, that many first year students have difficulty getting academically oriented, that new-found independence can be distracting, that time management presents challenges, and so forth. Responding to these types of racist comments is important because any corrective, even the smallest comment, might have an impact on someone's attitudes and perceptions.

Replying to unwanted praise—
"You're such a good person"

Our estimation skills would be taxed if we tried to determine how many times we have been complimented for being such "good people" because we adopted African American children or how "lucky" our children are that we adopted them. Many adoptive parents receive this type of praise from others, but we sense that the tributes that come our way are magnified because our children are black. We have always responded to the "good people/lucky children" compliments with comments such as, "These children enrich our lives so much" or "We're the lucky ones to have these children in our family."

The "good people/lucky children" dynamic calls attention to a host of conflicting narratives about adoption, especially adoption by white parents of children of color. Adoption circumstances and the many stories that evolve over time about each and every adoption include elements ranging from violence to abandonment to abuse to death. Children who are adopted are anything but lucky because of the circumstances that have parted them from their birth parents. It's completely understandable, then, that adoption is seen as a lucky happening in contrast to the alternative of a child without a permanent family. Adoptive parents, knowing the circumstances of their child's life at the time of placement, legitimately feel that they are doing something good *for the child* and not just for themselves. Adopted children, as they mature and come to understand more aspects of their adoption story will develop different views about how adoption relates to what they know of their pre-adoption situation. Some adopted children will consider themselves lucky to have been given the life they have. Others will feel robbed of what they conceptualize as a lost family, community, and/or culture. Still others will experience feelings of both loss and luck, sometimes simultaneously and sometimes at different points in time. It's important for adoptive parents and adopted children to face their feelings honestly, and for parents to be supportive of their children, regardless of their feelings about loss or luck.

One of the more difficult situations when the good person/lucky child comments are made is when the child is facing problems in school, with peers, with drugs, with the legal system, or with physical or psychological health. "You've done everything you could...given this child's x, y, and z..." Sometimes there's a tone attached to messages like this when they are about adopted children rather than biological children. Well-meaning, sympathetic people make insensitive and inappropriate comments about what are seen as problem children, but such comments about an adopted child of color are especially potent. Perhaps comments are made that the "good parent" did not expect to get this kind of child, or even worse, comments suggesting that this might have been expected if you adopted a black child born to a teenage mother, or a Hispanic child who was taken into foster care because of abuse in the home, or a child who was relinquished by the parent and is in an orphanage in Taiwan. In every case, it is important for parents to remind those who take pity or who somehow position the adopted child as "damaged goods" that *no family is immune from children who have problems.* That is the dynamic underlying the response that we believe in for the good person/lucky child comments: we, the parents, are the lucky ones because we have this child or these children.

Whatever the dynamic inside a family about stories and feelings of loss and luck and about the importance of love to nurture a child, it is not healthy for the external view of the child as *so lucky* and the parents as *so good* to be the controlling narrative. Most people who decide to adopt a child do so after considerable introspection, conversations, and consultations. Adoptive parents want to be parents and to have their families enriched by the presence of children. Adopted children need to be bolstered as much as possible to see themselves as persons of individual merit and not as children who were rescued. It is especially important that your child does not hear comments that suggest he or she is pitied or felt sorry for. When adopted children are ready and want to discuss how they feel about the loss—luck—love interplay, it is for them to choose how, when, and with whom to have the conversation.

The importance of stories— *"Once upon a time…"*

In this chapter, we've stressed the ways in which talking with others about your plans to adopt and about your adopted children of color can present challenges. Our intent has been to focus on what we hope will be helpful advice about how to think through and anticipate some of these challenges. There are no hard and fast rules for how to handle the many instances in which comments and actions require responses from white parents of children of color, but a guiding set of principles helps untangle what can seem a snarl of issues. What we've learned over time—and sometimes in hindsight—is that many of the difficult situations and delicate topics can be anticipated.

Others, of course, come as a surprise and offer additional learning opportunities that may be helpful in future situations.

In all of our advice and commentary in this chapter, the issue of the adopted child's story is critical. *The child's story is the child's to share and tell.* This does not mean that parents should be completely silent. As the child grows and matures, learning more about the circumstances of her or his adoption, more can be shared with others. Because there are no hard and fast rules, there may also be circumstances in which an adoptive parent decides that communication with others is important. If a child has a disability, there may be good reason to talk about aspects of the child's background with other parents who face similar challenges. For single adoptive parents, it may be important to have trusted confidants simply because it can be difficult to hold everything to yourself. At some point, a story will settle in that can be told, but that story may change over time, even as your child reaches adulthood. What details should be shared, for instance, about a choice to search for birth parents? Or details about birth parents known either because the adoption was open or a search has located a birth parent and birth family? Professionals in adoption agencies and many resources that are now available online can offer help in making a myriad of decisions and choices about communication with others, but even these do not replace clear and frank communication with your adopted son or daughter.

Things to consider

- *Well-meaning people say the darndest things!* If you're thinking about adopting a child of a different race, are in the process, or have already done so, be prepared to field a lot of questions from family, friends, acquaintances, and even strangers about your interest and motives. Remember that it's YOU and not they making this important decision about adoption.

- *Racism can catch you off guard.* Sometimes people ask questions or say things about race that take your breath away. Breathe deeply before responding. Work to answer directly and—whenever possible—without alienating the other person. Don't let the question or comment pass without any response.

- *Be careful responding to "You're such a good [white] person."* Because so many children awaiting adoption are from difficult circumstances, a white person who is considering or has adopted a child of color will often be highlighted as a good person for taking in a lucky child. This response is understandable, but it's important to highlight yourself as fortunate to be creating a family across race. Even more important is identifying the child as welcomed, loved, and not rescued.

- *Your child's story is private and not completely yours to tell.* Adoptive parents are often tempted to tell *their* story, which includes the details of their adopted child's birth and birth family circumstances. At every stage of development, it's critical to an adopted child's identity that she or he decide whether to disclose sensitive details. A child should never learn for the first time about something from their placement story that they haven't heard from their adoptive parents.

- *Not all racially focused comments and questions are intentionally racist.* Try to meet others with an eye toward constructive engagement. Institutional racism deeply penetrates many aspects of our lives and our perceptions in ways that are out of our awareness.

References

Centers for Disease Control and Prevention (2011) *Attention Deficit Hyperactivity Disorder Among Children Aged 5–17 Years in the United States, 1998–2009.* NCHS Data Brief, No. 70. Available at www.cdc.gov/nchs/data/databriefs/db70. pdf, accessed on 7 February 2013.

"Driving While Black." (2008) Television segment from UPN9-New York posted on *YouTube,* 18 August. Available at www.youtube.com/watch?v=jcanTRJjDAI, accessed on 7 February 2013.

Keefer, B. and Schooler, J.E. (2000) *Telling the Truth to Your Adopted or Foster Child— Making Sense of the Past.* Westport, CT: Bergin & Garvey.

Spickard, P. and Daniel, G.R. (eds) (2004) *Racial Thinking in the United States: Uncompleted Independence.* Notre Dame, IN: University of Notre Dame Press.

Staples, B. (2009) "Even Now, There's Risk in 'Driving While Black'." *New York Times,* 14 June, p. A20.

Wiley, K. (2012) "Stop pretending racism is over." *The Boston Globe,* 14 July, p. A11.

Resources

Brown, S., Cuckens, B., Maslowski, J. and Rupp, L. (2012) "Why do you ask?" *Adoptive Families. Available at www.adoptivefamilies.com/articles.php?aid=1758.*
This article offers four different personal accounts of intrusive questions and comments about adoption and how they were dealt with, as well as a number of comments in response to the article.

Krueger, A. (2009, June 4) "Positive adoption language." Available at *http://suite101. com/article/positive-adoption-language-a122829.*
Angela Krueger provides clean guidance on terms to use when talking about adoption. She also has posts on helping kids answer questions about adoption and other related topics.

Stern-LaRosa, C. and Hofheimer Bettmann, E. (2000) *The Anti-Defamation League's Hate Hurts: How Children Learn and Unlearn Prejudice.* New York: Scholastic Inc.
This ADL book includes information on how children perceive difference, stories about responses to hateful words and behavior, and guidelines that are helpful for challenging biased materials in settings ranging from schools to mass media. The ADL website contains other useful perspectives related to race and prejudice: *www.adl.org.*

CHAPTER 3

Helping Your Child Develop a Healthy Racial Identity—

"Daddy, Why Am I Brown and You're Pink?"

Children see difference at a very young age and they develop attitudes about those differences. Racial attitudes, especially racial prejudice, are found in very young children. Social scientists are unsure about how perceptions of race and ethnicity develop in children, but they are certain that it does, and that those perceptions have material consequences for children of color. Because your child's racial identity will significantly affect his or her life, relationships, and access to money, jobs, housing, and other resources, it is critical that you help your child develop a healthy racial identity.

This chapter examines why a healthy racial identity is important and provides suggestions for ways that parents can help children develop a healthy racial identity. It also looks at specific strategies for incorporating your child's racial and cultural background into your everyday lives. We'll look first at the stages of racial identity development and why racial identity is important.

The development of racial identity—*"Who am I?"*

Personal identity is complex. As individuals we are the products of multiple factors. Our families, our peers, our teachers, where we live, the media we consume, our gender, our ethnicity, our race, our personal experiences, and numerous other factors intersect in unique ways to create our personal identity. There is no formula, however, that can predict how these factors will affect any one individual. But we do know that they affect us to some degree and in some way. Race affects all of us. Although many whites do not think of themselves as having a race and are not, therefore, likely to acknowledge that their race has consequences for their lives, people of color are very aware that race matters. Marlene recalls facilitating a dialogue on race and ethnicity among a small group of professionals in Boston in which a white female participant commented that race had not come up once in a conversation that she had with another white member of the dialogue group when they were processing a group exercise. She concluded that race was really not an important dimension of most people's daily lives. Marlene turned to a black man in the group and asked him if he had talked about race in relation to the exercise with his discussion partner, also a black man. He said yes. And then he looked at everyone in the group and said, "I think about race every day. And my black friends and I talk about race every day." The white woman seemed stunned by his comment. The interchange points to the enormous divide between the experiences of whites and people of color and to the need for white parents of children of color to ensure that their children develop a healthy racial identity.

Although social scientists do not agree on how racial identity develops, they are able to identify the stages children go through in developing their racial identity. Stephen Quintana (1998) reviewed hundreds of studies on the development of racial identity in children and concluded that there are four developmental stages. Knowing the stages helps parents understand what your children are experiencing, why they say or do particular things, and how you can respond to your children in constructive ways.

Stage 1—"You're not white, you're pink"

The first stage occurs in children who are three to six years old. At this stage of development, children experience race visually and describe it literally. One of our sons was washing his hands with Marlene when he around four years old and closely examined his hands and her hands. He was already familiar with the terms "black people" and "white people" and as he looked back and forth at their hands, he said, "Mommy, my skin isn't black, it's brown. And your skin is pink, not white." That comment is typical for children that age. Very young children are unaware of the racial connotations of "black." To them, black (or in the example above, brown) is a term that describes someone's skin color—no more, no less. In fact, references to black people and white people are probably confusing to children because their references for skin color names are most likely names given to the colors of the crayons and markers that they use to draw pictures of people.

That race is only a set of physical characteristics for very young children doesn't mean, however, that parents should ignore questions about race or not talk with young children about race. Quintana (1998) suggests that at this age parents should make sure that their children understand that race is not a taboo subject. If parents keep the lines of communication about race open, then children will be able to develop more nuanced understandings of race as they get older. Marlene remembers picking up our older son from preschool one day when a black child loudly asked, "Who are you?" When she replied that she was our son's mother, the child responded, "You can't be his mommy; you're white and he's black." Marlene hesitated for a moment and then realized that the child's comment showed no malice, just curiosity. She smiled and said, "I adopted him." The young boy said, "Oh, okay."

Stage 2—"All my Chinese friends play the violin. Chinese people must be good at it"

As children get older (six to ten years), they develop concrete operational thinking and the ability to take the perspective of another person. With the development of these abilities, children begin to shift their understanding of race from observable, physical characteristics to non-observable, inferred characteristics. For example, rather than simply observing that white people live in big houses, they might say, "White people have important jobs and earn lots of money." This move to inferential thinking about race marks the second stage of racial identity formation. At this stage, Quintana advises parents to help their children learn about the history of their racial group and to learn about differences in language, customs, and behaviors among racial and ethnic groups. He also warns parents that children in this developmental stage have difficulty understanding prejudice and they are troubled if they experience or witness prejudice. When our older son was in the second grade, his teacher did a unit on slavery as part of Black History month. That evening, the mother of his best friend, an Iranian boy, called us to say that her son had been sobbing non-stop since he returned from school. She said her son was overwhelmed by the realization that our son, his best friend, was black, just like the people who were slaves. He couldn't understand how white people could do those awful things to black people, particularly to his friend. We and the friend's parents talked with the teacher the next day, both to let her know how much the discussion about slavery had upset the child and to talk with her about how she planned to handle the situation. She was clearly at a loss, with no understanding that the subject matter might be disturbing to children this age. The incident made us aware for the first time how seemingly supportive words or actions, in this case a lesson plan aimed at teaching children about an important part of U.S. history, could easily prove hurtful if they are not grounded in an understanding of children's developmental understanding of race. Our point is not that elementary age children should not learn about slavery in school, but that teachers need to be prepared for the emotional consequences of the lesson and have strategies ready for dealing with them.

Stage 3—"Timmy said black people are dumb"

The third stage of racial identity development occurs between 10–14 years of age, when a child's social cognition develops. At this point, children begin to understand the rules and concepts that govern social interaction, and their own identities are heavily influenced by how they believe other people perceive them. Children at this stage are more likely to comment on social class differences and see those differences among ethnic groups. Because we tend to merge race and social class in the U.S., children at this age begin to perceive being black as being poor. Children also begin to see prejudice at this age and to be sensitive to the possibility of prejudice. That means that parents need to have an open and honest attitude toward the possibility of prejudice and not be defensive or minimize the point if or when your child tells you that they've experienced or seen someone else experience prejudice.

Not being defensive about racial prejudice is harder than you might think for most white people. As we said in Chapter 1, not having to think about race is one of the "privileges" of being white. When we're forced to think about it, in this case because our child talks with us about experiencing racism, we often become defensive for a number of reasons. First, most whites don't see much of the prejudice that blacks experience, either because we're not present when it happens or because we're "blind" to the slight. For example, a white woman in a workshop on cultural differences in the workplace that Marlene was facilitating shared an incident that had completely perplexed her. She was on a hiring committee that had interviewed several candidates. In the discussion following the interviews, she commented to the other members of the committee that the African American candidate, a woman, was "extremely articulate." The black members were enraged, and told her that her comment was racist. She didn't understand why. Marlene explained that African Americans have historically been labeled as using "deficient" or "non-standard" speech and that whites often describe blacks as being less articulate. In that context, singling out a black woman for being articulate implies that you didn't expect her to be able to speak well—an implication that most African Americans would find racist. Second, whites in the U.S. most often see racism as interpersonal in nature; blacks, on the other hand, define racism more broadly, seeing both its interpersonal and its institutional manifestations. When blacks accuse whites of racism they are often pointing to institutional examples; the accusation isn't intended as a personal affront but rather as a call for action to remedy the structural cause. In response, however, whites tend to take the accusation personally and become defensive.

Finally, it's very difficult when your child tells you about a racist incident not to be defensive. Whites carry a lot of guilt about the history and legacy of racism in the U.S. and that guilt can be paralyzing. It's hard to acknowledge the existence of racism without indicting ourselves as members of the same racial group that perpetuates it. For our children's sake, however, it's important to leave the guilt behind as much as possible and respond directly and non-defensively. Your child needs you to acknowledge their experience and feelings. If it was a situation in which they could have spoken up or reported what happened to an adult, then you can help them think about how to do so in the future.

Stage 4—"I'm going to wear my hair in corn rows"

The last stage in the development of racial identity occurs during adolescence, when your child is a teenager. At this stage, young people are less dependent on the views of others. They begin to look for "consistency, themes and self-identities that are generalizations of self across time, situations, and conflicting characteristics" (Quintana 1998, p.39). Teens often begin to actively express a racial or ethnic identity and to identify those who are in the group and those who are out of the group. As your child's racial/ethnic group consciousness develops, you need to acknowledge racial/ethnic group differences. At the same time, you need to refute racial stereotypes that you know are untrue, for example, black men are violent, Asians are good at math, or Latinos are lazy. Although teenagers frequently use stereotypes, especially when they are talking about other teens, they are cognitively capable of understanding how stereotypes are created and how to refute them. The key is to refute stereotypes but acknowledge cultural differences among groups, for instance, African American culture values community, Latino/a cultures value family, or Asian cultures value hierarchy. And you should support your child's expressions of racial or ethnic identity. When one of our sons was in high school, he let his hair grow long so that he could wear it braided. As his hair grew, it became more difficult for him to keep it groomed. We reminded ourselves daily how important it was to show our approval of what he was doing rather than discourage him. He decided to have his hair done in twists before it was long enough for braids, and discovered that longer styles took a great deal of time and cost a lot of money. When his twists fell out after a week, he returned to the barber's chair. But he looked terrific with twists, and he was pleased that he had tried it. His experimentation with his hair was only the start of his continuing expression of his African American identity.

In the remainder of this chapter, we explore ways that you can help your child develop a positive racial identity within your family. Before we do, however, we need to say something about the responsibility white parents of black children have to teach our children about very specific aspects of racism that they are likely to encounter. When our sons were young, black friends sometimes expressed concern that we might not be able to teach our sons how to behave when confronted by certain kinds of racist situations. For example, we learned from one set of black parents that they had not allowed their older son to drive until they were comfortable that he knew how to conduct himself if he were pulled over by the police (see the discussion in Chapter 2 on "driving while black"). They said their son had a hot temper and they were concerned that he wouldn't be what they called "properly deferential" if he were pulled over by the police. We followed their advice and had the same talk with our sons. Long before Trayvon Martin's hoodie became a national symbol of racial profiling, both of us had heard stories from black male students about being rounded up by the police when they were looking for a "young black man in a hoodie." The targeting of blacks, especially black men, by the police is a reality in many communities. Black parents, because they have experienced these situations themselves or have friends and family who have, understand their responsibility to teach their children how to respond in ways that will keep them safe. White parents of black children need to learn that lesson also.

Teaching our children about their racial identity, however, is not only about racism. It's also about the celebration of the unique aspects of their cultural heritage.

Incorporating your child's cultural heritage into your family—*The black angel on the Christmas tree*

Racial identity is not monolithic. The lived experiences of people of color vary greatly within racial groups in the U.S. and throughout the world. When our older child was six weeks old, we brought him with us to a party at the home of friends from Clark University. One of the guests was a black African man who grew up in France and was a senior producer with National Public Radio. Marlene, who was holding our son at the time, had an intense conversation with him about racial identity and our angst about whether we could introduce our son to experiences with African Americans in the inner city that would ensure he had a strong self-image as an African American man. After listening to Marlene's fears, he smiled and said, "You Americans are so strange. Why do you think African American identity is found only in inner city ghettos?" He pointed out that black experience varies across countries and cultures, and he concluded that our son's culture would be the culture we created for him in our family.

His comments made us reexamine not only our assumptions about what is African American culture and where we would find it, but also our definition of our child's culture. The issue was not simply how to introduce him to African American culture, but how we, as a family, would incorporate features of the culture of his birth into our lives in ways that felt authentic to us as a family. When you adopt a child of color, you remain a white person but you are now a white person in a multiracial family. Your identity has changed. As you think about creating a healthy racial identity for your child, you need to do that in the context of creating your family's racial identity. One of the ways of doing that is by creating family traditions that honor your child's cultural background.

As we proceeded through the adoption process, we met several other lesbian couples that had already adopted a child of color or were expecting to bring home a child very soon. They had formed an informal adoption group and asked us to join. The idea of the group was that we would meet at least several times each year, giving our children an opportunity to grow up knowing that there were other families like theirs and giving the parents an opportunity to share their experiences about parenting in general and parenting a child of color more specifically. Most of the children are grown now, and we've attended high school and college graduation parties and the first wedding in the group. We've also met other adoptive parents who have been members of similar adoption groups centered on their children's background, be it Chinese, Hispanic, or African American. All of them say that the support of the other families in their group has been very helpful. We write more about this in Chapter 6.

We created a lot of wonderful traditions in our adoption group—a yearly camping trip to the seashore, fall outings in western Massachusetts (where two of the families lived), yearly photographs of the children together so that we could chart their growth. The tradition most beloved by the children, however, was our annual Kwanzaa party.

Kwanzaa, an African American and Pan-African holiday created by Dr. Maulana Karenga, is celebrated from December 26 through January 1. Kwanzaa originates in ancient African first-fruit harvest celebrations; the contemporary version celebrates family, community, and culture, which makes it a perfect holiday in which members of any religious group and those who are not religious believers can participate. The celebration includes a candle lighting ceremony in which a new candle is lit each night. Because we would gather for a yearly Kwanzaa party, we lit all of the candles at once, with each candle lit by one child. Initially, the parents lit the candles and read the text about each concept. As the children got older, they began to take over the roles. Even if it was impossible to have our party during the exact Kwanzaa dates, we met every year to uphold the tradition.

The values represented by Kwanzaa are universal. As the children lit each candle, we would ask them what they thought each of the principles meant. The discussions deepened over the years as their understanding of the world grew larger, but each discussion became part of a growing foundation of knowledge each child had about African American culture. The experience was multilayered for all us. We simultaneously shared an opportunity to teach our children about their shared heritage; to celebrate family and connection, which were things we all valued; and to create a unique variation on Kwanzaa, one which would remain with our children always and would be something they could choose to pass down to their children.

We also used other religious celebrations as opportunities to incorporate African American culture into our lives. Our family celebrated both Hanukkah and Christmas. Marlene was raised in a Conservative Jewish family and Fern in a Lutheran family, but Marlene's commitment to her religion was stronger, so we both agreed that the boys would be raised as Jews. Christmas remained an important holiday to Fern, however, and Marlene loved the traditions of Christmas, so we had celebrated the holiday even before we had children. We did so, however, in a way that honored our family. Fern created a gold Jewish star that sat atop the tree each Christmas until our older son joined us. That year, a close friend gave us the black angel that had been on her family's tree when she was a child. The black angel replaced the Jewish star at the very top of the tree, but the star remained in a place of honor just below.

We also incorporated African American culture into traditional Jewish celebrations. We regularly celebrated Passover with a large gathering of friends, both Jewish and non-Jewish. The Passover story is about the Jewish people's exodus from slavery in Egypt and their journey to Israel, which represented a land of freedom. The story was perfect for including poems, prayers, and stories about slavery in the U.S. We transformed the traditional toast of "next year in Jerusalem," which refers to all Jews being free in Israel, into a call for freedom for all people throughout the world.

When the boys were preparing for their bar mitzvahs, the traditional Jewish ceremony that marks a 13-year-old boy's transition to being an adult member of the Jewish community (the term is bat mitzvah for girls), Marlene approached the rabbi of her Reform congregation about the possibility of including some traditional African American spirituals in the service, along with poems by Langston Hughes and Gwendolyn Brooks, well-known African American poets. The rabbi agreed. Not all rabbis would be so willing to incorporate such changes. But Marlene also did some research and discovered that several well-known spirituals were claimed by both Jews and African Americans. *Go Down Moses*, for example, which is usually included in the service that accompanies the Passover meal, was also sung by black slaves in the U.S. She found a recording of traditional black spirituals by a renowned Jewish chorus and shared it with the rabbi and the music director of the synagogue. Both of our sons had bar mitzvah ceremonies that celebrated their shared Jewish and African American identities. In addition to the ceremony drawing together their cultures, the boys also looked like African Jews. Several years before, Marlene's parents had bought each of them handmade Ethiopian yarmulkes, the traditional Jewish skullcaps worn by male members of a Jewish congregation. With the colorful caps perched proudly on their heads and the traditional Jewish "tallit" (prayer shawls) around their shoulders, the boys, as one friend commented, each looked like an African prince standing before family and friends and claiming his place in the community.

Religious ceremonies and celebrations are not the only opportunities you have to create family traditions that incorporate your child's cultural heritage. You could attend a local community breakfast every year on Martin Luther King's birthday, celebrate the Chinese New Year, or participate in other festivals that represent your child's heritage. What's important is ensuring that aspects of your child's heritage become part of your family's culture in ways that are natural, seamless, and enduring. The sociological literature calls this incorporation of a child's native group identity into the family's identity "culture keeping" (Jacobson 2008).

Creating your home—
"Black people live here too"

Parents-to-be often spend hours considering the ways they will prepare their home for the arrival of a child. What color should we paint the nursery or bedroom? What furniture should we purchase? Should the baby sleep in a cradle or a crib? Do we need special dishes and silverware? When we received a phone call letting us know that our older son was ready for us to pick him up, we were unprepared. The placement happened much more quickly than we expected, so we hadn't purchased any of the necessary items. Luckily, the sister of a close friend offered to give us the crib and cradle her children, now teenagers, had used. We also quickly purchased an infant car seat to take with us on our flight to pick up the baby, along with a car load of other stuff.

From that moment on, we had a clear idea about the items we needed to buy for our son. What we didn't know about, or didn't even consider, were things that he (and we) would need in order to identify our home as a place where blacks as well as whites live, especially as he grew older. Our home looked like the homes of most white people. We didn't have a single piece of art either by a black artist or with the image of a black person, a figurine or sculpture of a black person, or a piece of cloth with an African print. Both of us loved jazz, so we did have a large collection of CDs by African American musicians, and we had opera and classical recordings by black artists. Because we are academics who study race, we had many books by and about African Americans, and numerous volumes of literature, poetry, and plays by African Americans. Nothing else in our home, however, reflected any part of our son's cultural heritage.

Not having to think about how to create a physical and visual environment that includes your child's cultural heritage is another one of the privileges that white parents of white children carry in their knapsack of privileges. Once you are the parent of a child of color that privilege disappears. We don't mean to suggest, however, that having to think about decorating your home with items that reflect your child's cultural heritage, or playing music, preparing food, and reading books from your child's culture are a burden. Quite the opposite. We both learned so much about African American culture as we began to acquire items and do things that would help our sons see their cultural heritage in our home—and help us transform ourselves into members of a multicultural family. What we learned was exciting and joyful but also sometimes sobering.

For example, for our first Christmas with our older son we decided to buy some ornaments for the tree that would help our son see himself reflected in the images. We had the black angel from our friend, and we started looking for new ornaments to add to our collection. We searched the local Christmas stores, department stores, drug stores—finding nothing. No black Santa, no black angel, no black elves. The next year we were shopping in Chicago in the now defunct Marshall Field's department store when we encountered a Christmas tree display that included black ornaments. We quickly purchased several. We had been naïve to assume that we would find black ornaments in stores where we lived. We found them in Chicago because middle-class blacks with purchasing power lived there. The Boston suburbs were then and remain now primarily white. Over the years, we added more ornaments, ceramic figurines, art work, and other pieces to our collection of African American representations, purchasing them whenever we saw them, and learning how to seek them out. It seems naïve to say that it never occurred to us initially to ask African American friends where they shopped for Christmas ornaments or birthday cards with African Americans on them, but it didn't. Today, of course, you can buy these items wherever you live as long as you have access to the internet. But their unavailability in many communities speaks volumes about the separation of the races in the U.S., and about how difficult it is for children of color to grow up with the images that are so necessary to their developing a healthy racial identity.

It's important to note here that we are not calling for parents to purchase and consume objects from their child's native culture as if they were simply traveling through a foreign country. Pamela Quiroz, a sociologist who has studied the discourse of adoptive parents of Chinese and Guatemalan children, argues that "culture keeping" is "more aptly characterized as *cultural tourism*, the selective appropriation and consumption of renovated cultural symbols, artifacts, and events that serve as the sources of identity construction for adopted children" (Quiroz 2012, p.527). She found that many white adoptive parents gave their children experiences and objects from their native cultures in order to help their children develop a connection with those cultures, but refused to see their own identities changing in response to the consumption of those experiences and objects. As we said earlier in this chapter, you want to introduce aspects of your child's native culture into your family culture in ways that are authentic, natural, and enduring for *your family*, not just your child.

There are other things that parents need to have at home to help children of color see their images reflected back. Our colleagues hosted a baby shower after the arrival of each of the boys. We received numerous copies of *Goodnight Moon* and *The Runaway Bunny*, two books that both boys adored. We appreciated even more, however, the books we received that were about African American children or African folk tales, or included images of paintings by African American artists. Having books that feature black characters is critical for a black child, as are books with Asian children for a Korean or Chinese child. Books are one of the first places where children see themselves reflected back to themselves. Fortunately, there are more books available today than 20 years ago, and parents can easily order those books online.

Other media are important also. Television shows like *Sesame Street* have long provided diverse characters for children to see, but many other shows do not. Parents need to ensure that children have an opportunity to watch children's shows that include children of color. When children are old enough to go to the movies, or when you show them videos at home, make sure that they see positive characters of color, and that you talk with your children when the images on the screen are troublesome.

Providing opportunities for children of color to see positive representations of members of their race or ethnicity is doubly important because they will be exposed to many representations that are not positive. For example, Disney films are one of the major sources of negative representations of people of color. Whether it's the King Louie monkey in *The Jungle Book* (a character who sounds suspiciously like Louis Armstrong) who sings "I wanna be like you" to the white boy or Uncle Remus, the old black man happily working on a plantation in the post-Civil War South in *Song of the South*, or the jive talking black crows in *Dumbo* or the scheming hyenas who use African American dialect in *The Lion King*, Disney films are filled with negative images of people of color generally and blacks in particular. Even Disney's recent animated feature, *The Princess and the Frog*, which features Disney's first black princess, Princess Tiana, includes racist images. Princess Tiana's fairy godmother resembles a black mammy, and a Haitian medicine man in the movie wears an African mask and dabbles in voodoo. Princess Tania herself spends most of her time on camera as a frog.

It's virtually impossible, however, to keep a child from seeing Disney films. They dominate at the box office; are shown frequently on television, especially on the Disney Channel or ABC, which is owned by Disney; and appear in virtually every family's collection of DVDs. Many of the films and their characters' images are iconic in American culture so any child unfamiliar with them is at a distinct disadvantage.

Because Disney is ubiquitous, instead of trying to keep your children from seeing the movies, you can watch them with your children and query them to see what beliefs, ideas, or attitudes they are taking away from them. You can then correct any misperceptions they might have. For example, in *Aladdin*, an Arab shopkeeper threatens to cut off Princess Jasmin's hand because she takes an apple from his shop and gives it to a poor person on the street. The film teaches children that this is how Arabs deal with stealing. That lesson, however, is untrue. The Koran says that you should feed the poor, so Princess Jasmin was justified in taking the apple and she would not be punished under Islamic law. Disney films are captivating and enjoyable for young and old. Watching them with your children can be both fun and educational—as long as you, not Disney, do the educating.

Creating opportunities for shared learning—*"Did you know that W.E.B. Dubois helped found the NAACP?"*

When the boys were young, we purchased a set of knowledge cards titled *African American Wisdom*. Each card in the set had a wood block portrait of a famous African American on one side of the card and a brief biography of the person on the other side. The deck included artists, poets, writers, sports figures, social activists, and politicians. The cards were a fun way for us to learn about African American history together, and the boys also learned that there were many important African Americans in whom they could take great pride.

We also encouraged the boys to use school assignments as opportunities to learn about African American history. When one of our sons was asked to write a biography of a famous person, he chose Jackie Robinson. The assignment allowed him to learn about not only Jackie Robinson the baseball star but also Jackie Robinson the man who broke the color line in baseball. That meant that he read about the Negro Leagues, about segregation in the south (Robinson couldn't stay in the same hotels as his white teammates when they were on the road), and about racism generally in the U.S. in the late 1940s. In high school, one of our sons wrote a paper comparing rap music and certain Jewish prayers as forms of social protest. As you will see in Chapter 5, both boys used the ubiquitous "family tree" assignment to learn more about African American history.

We also used our nightly dinner conversations to talk about not only things we did that day but also people and events in the news. Those conversations were easy and interesting ways to engage the boys in conversations about race and racism and to identify successful African Americans in politics, business, sports, and the arts. Election season is a good time to talk about the dearth of African Americans in political life in the U.S. Why, for example, have only six African Americans been elected to the U.S. Senate? As we write this chapter in 2012, there are ZERO African Americans in the Senate and only two Latino and two Asian Pacific senators. These topics are natural ways to talk with your children about race.

Black hair and skin—*"Are you keeping that baby's hair?"*

When our older son arrived home with us he had a head full of baby fine, softly curled hair. Black friends told us that the tradition in the black community was to wait one year before cutting his hair. And then they told us that his hair would not grow back baby fine and softly curled. Instead, he would have a nappy head of hair—thick, coarse, and tightly curled. That information was invariably followed by, "You remember to keep his hair," which was not an admonition about keeping his baby hair as a memento, but about making sure that his hair always looked good.

Looking good—hair neat, clothes clean, shoes shined—is an important cultural value for many in the African American community. In her memoir about growing up black in Minneapolis in the 1960s, Michele Norris, an African American journalist, writes about her mother's admonition to her family that, "You never know who's watching" (Norris 2010, p.86). Norris says that regardless of where they were or what they were doing—at home or in public—"We always looked put together. Hair pressed. Clothes ironed. Shoes spit-polished… We didn't just emulate the all-American white families in the Coca-Cola commercials—we tried to top them" (pp.40–41). Keeping a black child's hair, however, is not easy, especially if you are unfamiliar with the particular quirks of African American hair and the procedures and products for caring for it.

Shortly before we adopted our first son, we attended an adoption conference, where we participated in a workshop on taking care of African American hair. When we walked into the room, an African American beautician was vigorously combing through the hair of a young African American girl while her white mother looked on. The beautician was muttering about how tangled the child's hair was, and how it had clearly not been "taken care of." Taking care of it, we learned, meant brushing it every day, even if your child screamed that it hurt (the child in the room was doing just that). We also learned that African American hair tends to be very dry so it needs to be heavily moisturized each day. African American skin is also often very dry, which leads to an ashy color if it's not properly moisturized. The workshop helped prepare us for taking care of our sons' hair and skin. But it was only the beginning.

When our sons were young, Fern cut their hair using a professional set of electric clippers and she always breathed a sigh of relief when black friends said that their hair looked good. Our older son was a good sport about submitting to Fern and the clippers. Our younger son, on the other hand, did not appreciate the hot blades on his scalp. Hair-cutting day was torture, for him and for us. When the boys were about six and eight, Fern said that she was putting away the clippers; it was time to find a black barber. We had seen a barbershop with one black barber in a neighboring town, so we took the boys there. The boys declared that they preferred Fern to the black barber, so Fern brought the clippers back out. After a few months, it was clear that the boys were getting too old to not have their hair properly styled, so we asked an African American neighbor to recommend another black barber.

He did, and a few days later, Marlene took the boys to a barbershop in a nearby town. This time the shop had only African American barbers. It also had a very long line of customers. The boys and Marlene took their place in line and then waited for several hours until it was their turn. Waiting so long gave Marlene a lot of time to observe. The shop was obviously a neighborhood meeting place for men of color. Initially, only men were in the shop, but later in the afternoon, some women arrived with food for the barbers. People in the shop were having animated conversations. Often, a barber and his client would get into a heated disagreement about something and they would turn to the men and boys who were waiting and ask them to settle the disagreement. Our sons were included in those discussions.

They also received the same "in-group" handshake from their barber that the others had received—and even though neither had yet participated in such a handshake, they both figured it out. It was a remarkable experience for the boys; they received their first real "black" haircut, emerging with hair that had razor sharp lines all around their heads, along with an introduction to black male camaraderie. When Marlene and the boys left the barbershop, our younger son turned to her and said, "Mom, did you know that you were the only white person there?" Marlene paused, smiled, and said, "I knew." It was, of course, impossible not to know! Marlene had experienced for the first time in her life something that African Americans experience nearly every day of their lives: being the only person of her race in the room. It was humbling, and especially so because she had been given access to the warmth, playfulness, and generosity of the African American community from the inside.

The boys became regulars at that barbershop for the next 10 years. Even after we moved to a community about 20 miles away, we continued to drive the boys back for their haircuts. When they learned how to drive, they went themselves. Our trips to the barbershop were about more than getting a haircut; they were also important moments in the development of our sons' racial identities. The 2002 film *Barbershop*, starring Ice Cube and Cedric the Entertainer, takes viewers inside a day in the life of a South Side Chicago barbershop. The film is a comedy but also an accurate representation of the barbershop as a major center of black life in the neighborhood and of the importance of keeping and styling hair in the black community. Parents of African American girls can watch *Beauty Shop* (2005) with Queen Latifah, which provides similar insights into styling black women's hair.

It's important for whites to understand the centrality of the barbershop and beauty parlor as cultural spaces for blacks in the U.S. Many whites do recognize the church as a central community space for blacks. During the many years when blacks were denied access to most other cultural spaces—theaters, restaurants, gyms, tennis courts, golf courses, museums—the church became not only the spiritual center of the community but also its gathering place. Black barbershops and beauty parlors played a similar role in neighborhood life. They were places where blacks could gather safely, free to express themselves without worrying about how whites might see and judge them. They were also spaces where blacks could attend to how black hair grows and how it needs to be cut and styled, and where products necessary to maintain black hair were available. The barbershop and beauty parlor, like the black church, continue today to be locations for cultural connection.

Other hair and skin issues emerged over the years. One of our sons has the kind of beard that causes ingrown hairs and razor bumps, a condition that is common among African American men. After consulting a white dermatologist who had no idea how to treat the condition, we talked with our son's barber. He gave our son very specific instructions on how to handle the situation: which razor to use (which is actually not a razor but a hair trimmer used to style black hair), how to soften his beard before he shaved, how to treat his face afterwards. We tell this story not to provide instructions on how to deal with this particular condition but to emphasize the importance of not assuming that your child's grooming will be the same as yours. For example, teenagers often resist using sun screen when they are out in the sun, but it's doubly difficult to convince your dark-skinned children that they are in danger if they don't use sunscreen. Our experience also highlights the importance of finding doctors who either know about the particular medical conditions of your child's racial or ethnic group, or recognize that they need to ask questions and do research to find out about them.

Differences in skin and hair also create potential issues for white parents when their children of color want to change some aspect of their appearance in order to appear more "white." In

Chapter 1 we discussed *internalized racism*, which occurs when an individual begins to believe prejudiced ideas about themselves or others of their race. As children become more aware of their racial identity and how others see them as members of their race, there is the possibility that they will internalize negative ideas about themselves—*my skin is too dark, my eyes are too slanted, my nose is too broad.* Those internalized beliefs may lead them to want to change those aspects of their appearance by using skin cream that lightens their skin or even surgical procedures to release their eyelids or change the shape of their nose. These requests should be taken seriously by parents and not simply brushed away. They can be "teachable moments" for parents to talk with their children about ways that the culture teaches them to devalue themselves. They can also be learning moments for parents. When the black son of white friends was in college, he decided he wanted to have his beard permanently removed through laser treatment. Since he didn't have the money to afford it himself, he asked his parents to pay for it. They were initially shocked that he would consider such a drastic measure but after talking about it with several African American men, they learned that some black men choose laser hair removal to deal with their beard problems. Their son decided on his own that the procedure was too costly and difficult to pursue at that point in his life, but our discussions with our friends taught us about the seriousness of the skin problems faced by many black men.

Where to go on vacation— *"Are there any black folks there?"*

Another practical consideration for interracial families is where to go on vacation. Many of the vacation spots that white families frequent are not welcoming to people of color, and, even when they are, the absence of people of color can make your children (and you) uncomfortable. Our older son arrived home in the spring. In July, when he was four months old, we joined close friends for a vacation on the coast of Maine. We rented a vacation house on the water in a small fishing village and spent three weeks exploring the region. One evening during the second week of our vacation, we went to dinner with the baby in tow. As we entered the restaurant, several people greeted us as if they knew us. We said hello and, after we were seated at our table, we tried to remember where we had met them. We had no idea. Several days later, after a similar experience, a light bulb went off for us. Of course people recognized us. We were the only two white women there traveling with a black infant. In fact, we hadn't seen a black face other than our son's during our entire vacation. Several years later, we were visiting Fern's family in Minneapolis and decided to spend a week with our sons in northern Minnesota in a resort area that Fern's family knew well. We were sitting in an ice cream shop enjoying our sundaes, when our younger son peered around the shop and asked us if we had noticed that we hadn't seen any black people since we had arrived. We had seen a few Native Americans, but no blacks. That was the last time we took a vacation without thinking carefully about whether our children would feel welcome.

We knew that many middle-class African Americans vacationed on Martha's Vineyard, a small island 45 minutes by ferry off the coast of Massachusetts. One summer when the boys were relatively young, we took the ferry over for a day trip and the four of us biked around Oak Bluffs, the island town with the largest African American population and a long history as an African American vacation spot (Sege 2009; Nelson 2005). The boys' excitement when we arrived and saw so many black faces was palpable. We decided then that we would do summer vacations on the Vineyard as often as we could and were fortunate to receive advice about the island from black friends whose families had vacationed there for several generations.

Role models—*"Mirror mirror on the wall..."*

Positive role models who share your children's racial or ethnic identity are an important component of a healthy racial identity. Providing those role models can be difficult for white parents, however, unless they have an extensive array of friends and colleagues who have the same racial identity as their children. While we encourage you to become friends with people of color, we also recognize the difficulty of doing so (see our comments in Chapter 1 about "difficult dialogues") and we caution you to initiate such friendships only when they feel genuine to you. As with any advice we provide in this book, do only those things that are compatible with who you are. That doesn't mean that you shouldn't do things that take you out of your comfort zone—reaching across racial and ethnic differences can be uncomfortable at times—but what you do has to be consistent with your identity, albeit now your identity as a member of a multiracial family.

Although we did not have a wide circle of friends of color, we did have a number of close friends and colleagues to whom we could turn for advice and who served as role models for the boys. We also had the benefit of Fern's siblings, both of whom are married to people of another race. Our sons grew up knowing that they had a Korean aunt, a Hawaiian uncle of Chinese and Polynesian ancestry, and mixed-race cousins.

If you don't have friends and family who can be role models for your children, reaching out to teachers and community leaders of color is an option. Adults of color know how important it is for young people to have positive racial role models, and they are usually very willing to help white parents. Some of our friends, especially single women, who have adopted children of color have worked through the Big Brothers Big Sisters organization to find mentors for their children. Big Brothers Big Sisters is present in most major metropolitan areas in the U.S. and there are other similar mentoring programs throughout the country.

Of course children encounter many role models through media. The problem, however, is that not all of those role models are positive. Positive media representations of African Americans continue to be scarce. Instead, children consume media that portray blacks as criminals, hustlers, or objects of ridicule. Reality television especially glamorizes rappers and their over the top lifestyles. This glamorization of rap stars is complicated by the trend among many young whites, especially males, to look and act "ghetto." We've talked with many college students who report attending "ghetto" parties for whites only, where young white people dress "ghetto." We don't believe that these young people are necessarily being intentionally racist. Our students report that high school age white boys say being "ghetto" seems more exciting and courageous than being "white." When whites dress "ghetto," however, they are not assumed to *be* "ghetto." Others perceive them as playing a role. Blacks who dress "ghetto" are assumed to be poor, uneducated, and dangerous. For Asians and Hispanics, the media images are even scarcer, and what's there is mostly stereotypic. White parents need to be aware of the media images their children consume and the consequences if their children begin to imitate certain lifestyles.

Finally, keep in mind that you are the most important role model in your children's lives. Your words and actions are daily reminders to your children about how to stand up to racist or inappropriate comments. You can also be a positive role model by joining organizations that are committed to eliminating racism or that support people of color. You can work to elect candidates of color to political office locally or nationally. If the community groups that you are active in are not diverse, you can work to make them more inclusive. You will have many opportunities as parents to show your children that you don't just "talk the talk," you "walk the walk."

In the next chapter, where we discuss how to talk with your child about adoption and race, we continue to explore the development of racial identity. Then in Chapter 5, we discuss the ways adoption and race affect educational choices and practices for your child, and we provide practical information about choosing a school, talking with teachers, and affecting curriculum development.

Things to consider

- *Race matters.* A child needs a healthy sense of his or her racial identity in order to cope with the social and material consequences of race.

- *Racial identity is shaped by many factors.* You have multiple ways to ensure that your child can develop a healthy racial identity.

- *Keep an open and honest attitude about racial prejudice.* Try not to be defensive about being white.

- *Keep race in the conversation.* Make sure your child knows that you are always open to talking about race.

- *Remember that you are now a part of an interracial family.* Your child's racial identity is an integral part of your family identity, which means that your identity has also changed.

- *Create a home that says "black people live here too."* Be sure that your child sees himself or herself reflected in your home.

- *Be a positive role model for your child and commit to anti-racism work.* Show through what you do that you value diversity and are committed to unlearning racism and unmasking white privilege.

References

Jacobson, H. (2008) *Culture Keeping*. Nashville, TN: Vanderbilt University Press.

Nelson, J. (2005) *Finding Martha's Vineyard: African Americans at Home on an Island*. New York: Doubleday.

Norris, M. (2010) *The Grace of Silence*. New York: Vintage Books.

Quintana, S. (1998) "Children's developmental understanding of ethnicity and race." *Applied and Preventive Psychology 7*, 1, 27–45.

Quiroz, P.A. (2012) "Cultural tourism in transnational adoption: 'Staged authenticity' and its implications for adopted children." *Journal of Family Issues 33*, 4, 527–555.

Sege, I. (2009) "As the president gets ready to vacation on Martha's Vineyard, African-American families say it's a place they've loved for years, and where race isn't an issue." *The Boston Globe*, 15 August, p.G14.

Resources

Byrd, A. and Tharps, L. (2001) *Hair Story: Untangling the Roots of Black Hair in America*. New York: St. Martin's Press.
This book offers an historical overview of black hair, reaching back to 15th-century Africa and covering a broad range of issues and practices related to black hair from slave times to the present.

www.officialkwanzaawebsite.org.
This site provides information on Kwanzaa.

Tatum, B. (1997) *"Why Are All the Black Kids Sitting Together in the Cafeteria?" And Other Conversations About Race*. New York: Basic Books.
Tatum provides an in-depth and accessible treatment of the development of racial identity.

We have found personal memoirs to be an excellent source of information about racial and ethnic identities. There are many fine ones available. In addition to Michele Norris's *The Grace of Silence* (see citation under References), we especially like the following two books, both of which explore the conflicts and challenges of negotiating an identity that is shaped by more than one race, ethnicity, or culture.

Obama, B. (2004) *Dreams from My Father: A Story of Race and Inheritance*. New York: Broadway.
This was Barack Obama's first memoir. It focuses on his childhood and early adult life, providing a poignant picture of a young biracial man who tries to find his place in a world in which he never feels quite at home. Obama's analysis of race relations is insightful and powerful.

Lam, A. (2005) *Perfume Dreams*. Berkeley, CA: Heyday Books.
Lam, a journalist, recalls his family's emigration from Vietnam to the U.S. and his struggle, which includes a return to Vietnam, to find an identity that can encompass being both a Vietnamese son and an American.

CHAPTER 4

Talking about Race and Adoption with Your Child—

"Mommy, Who's My Real Daddy?"

When our sons were 9 and 11 we moved to a new community that was closer to the private school they were attending. To make the move more palatable to the boys, who didn't want to leave the house they had grown up in or their neighborhood friends, we promised to get them a dog. We all agreed that we would get a chocolate Labrador retriever, knowing that the breed was "family-friendly" but not knowing that chocolate Labs are often temperamentally difficult. Our dog, although we loved him dearly, turned out to be very challenging. The four of us attended "puppy kindergarten" with our dog in tow each week. And each session, the trainer chastised us for not being able to control the dog. One week, as we were waiting for the session to begin and the boys were off playing with the dog, we expressed our frustration with our dog's behavior to a woman whose dog was in the same class. She was a social worker, and after we finished our litany of complaints about the dog, she looked at us and said, "No matter how badly the dog behaves, you cannot give him back to the breeder. You have adopted children, and they might think that if dogs that behave badly can be given back, then maybe children who behave badly can be given back." Her words stayed with us—not just through our various trials with our dog (who did eventually become a wonderful family pet), but also as we considered other things that parents might say to an adopted child that could unintentionally be hurtful.

This chapter focuses on how to talk about both race and adoption with your children. Various resources provide good advice on how to talk to your children about adoption and also about race. Our purpose is not to repeat that advice but to help you think about how to talk to your child about race and adoption in the context of not sharing the same racial identity with your child. As we consider how to talk with your children about race and adoption, keep in mind the three types of racism we identified in Chapter 1: interpersonal racism (both physical and verbal), institutional racism, and internalized racism. Each of these is likely to be part of a conversation with your child at some point in their lives. Also keep in mind, the stages of racial identity that we described in Chapter 3. In talking about both race and adoption with your child, you need to consider where your child is developmentally with regard to understanding race. That point is aptly demonstrated in the following example from the newspaper advice column, "Dear Margo" (2012). A reader asks how to answer questions about sexuality that her children, ages four and six, are beginning to ask. "Margo" tells the reader to be honest and direct, but to remember that there is "a limit to what young children can take in when it comes to details" (p.G23). She recounts a story about a child who asks his mother where he came from and the mother begins a detailed explanation of sexual reproduction. The child interrupts and says, "No I mean, where did I come from? Timmy came from Cleveland" (p.G23). Although the example is about sex, the point is critical. Be honest and direct with your child, but keep your answers at their level of understanding.

Talking about adoption—
"Where did I come from?"

When we were growing up, adoption usually wasn't talked about. Adoptive parents rarely acknowledged publicly that their children were adopted, and often, even privately, kept that information from their children. We had a close friend early in our careers, an African American professor, who had a young son. We often told her that we thought her son looked more like her than her husband and she always agreed. Only after she died of cancer at a young age did her husband mention that their son was adopted. Pretending that a child is your biological offspring rather than adopted isn't possible, however, if your child is of another race. Even young children who don't yet understand how children are conceived and born "know" that a black child is not the birth child of white parents. Adoptive parents of a child of another race have no choice; they must talk about adoption with their child.

Talking about adoption is also a necessity in open adoptions, which are now more prevalent than closed adoptions, especially in the adoption of infants (Siegel and Smith 2012). The primary reason adoption used to be clouded in secrecy was that people believed that illegitimate births were shameful and infertility a taboo subject. Since most children placed into adoption were born to unwed mothers, adoption itself became a shameful secret. In recent years, adoption practices have changed. Many adoption professionals now believe that open adoptions—ones in which the birth mother (and occasionally the birth father) maintains some degree of contact with her birth child—help adopted children understand their identity, help adoptive parents better understand their children's needs, and help comfort birth mothers (Henry and Pollack 2009). Open adoptions vary in degree from one initial meeting with the birth mother along with sharing information and pictures to long-term periodic contact between the adoptive family and the birth mother.

Interracial adoptions that are open can provide an adopted child with good opportunities to learn about his or her birth culture, assuming, of course, that the birth mother or members of her extended family maintain contact with your family. They may also, however, be highly conflicted and painful for your child. Open adoptions may also be fraught with social class and/or cultural differences that are difficult to explain to a young child. We are not suggesting that we believe open adoptions are not good for children in interracial adoptions. Quite the opposite, in fact. We are saying, however, that adoptive parents need to be prepared for the particular issues that are brought to the fore in open adoptions, and how race will be a consideration.

Developmental stages in understanding adoption

Talking to your child about adoption is not as straightforward as it might seem. As with their understanding of race and racial identity, children's understanding of adoption develops over time. Lois Melina (2003) outlines four stages in a child's understanding of birth and adoption. When the race of the parent and child differ, additional issues will come up at each stage.

STAGE 1—"THIS IS MY FAMILY"

Preschool children don't differentiate between adoption and being born into a family. They accept being told that they are adopted or that a friend is adopted but they don't yet understand what adoption means. At this stage parents can lay the foundation for a child's future understanding. You can tell your child his or her "adoption story" at this stage and even create a picture book about it (sometimes called a "welcome home" book). We created a book for each of our sons. Our older son's book began with the two of us sitting on a beach in Italy dreaming about having a family and continues with the story of our journey to bring him home to our family. We included pictures of him arriving with us at the airport in Boston and pictures of family members and friends. Our younger son's book begins with our deciding to find a brother for our older son. His book also includes pictures of him with family members and friends. Initially we used the books to tell each of the boys the story of their adoption. As they grew older, they would take the book out and tell their stories to friends and family who would visit us. Even though they didn't "understand" in a concrete sense what it means to be adopted, they did know from an early age that they were each a member of a loving family that cherished them, and they learned to say, "I am adopted." The pictures in their books also gave us an opportunity to tell them additional stories about the family members and friends pictured in the books who, over the years, might not be physically present in our lives very often. Susan Tompkins (2011) suggests that parents play the adoption story with their children. For example, you and your young child can use dolls or stuffed animals to reenact the story and even use Lego blocks, Lincoln Logs, or other materials to build a hospital, orphanage, foster home, or other physical location important to the story. At this stage, adopted children of another race will have noticed or heard others comment on "the color difference." Even if your child does not understand the concepts involved, this is a time to begin simple statements about different kinds of families. For children who are adopted from other counties and will likely not be infants, there will be a recognition that something very important has changed—the place, the customs, the language.

STAGE 2—"WHOSE TUMMY WAS I IN?"

The second stage in children's understanding of birth and adoption occurs between the ages of five and seven, when children understand conception and can then distinguish between birth and adoption. At this age, an adopted child needs to know that they were in a woman's tummy and "born" to someone just as other children who are not adopted were born. Having this information makes a child feel normal. Talking about birth parents, however, is likely to lead to a discussion of why a child was adopted, not from the perspective of the adoptive parents, who have already shared that information in the child's adoption story, but from the perspective of the birth parents. And for children of color that discussion often introduces social and cultural issues related to race, social class, and culture of national origin, issues that a child is too young to understand fully but nonetheless needs to learn about in an age-appropriate way.

Melina cautions all adoptive parents to be sure to include references to the birth father in discussions about birth with an adopted child. In many instances, adoptive parents know little to nothing about the birth father of their child. Young women, especially poor women, often choose to give up their birth child because the birth father has abandoned them or has made it clear that he doesn't want to take any responsibility for the child. Unable to care for the child without help, birth mothers often choose to give up their child rather than raise the child alone. Oftentimes, adoptive parents find it easier to tell their child an adoption story that includes a birth mother but no birth father. In the absence of information, children (and adults) will create their own scenarios. Melina relates the story of a little girl who, when told an adoption story that included a birth mother but no birth father, decided that her adoptive father had impregnated her birth mother. Melina suggests that when the actual circumstances of a child's birth are unknown, parents can use "probably" in creating a birth and adoption story, and her view is that this story is an opportunity for parents to talk about conception as a loving process that takes place between a man and a woman.

We disagree with Melina on this last suggestion and offer a caveat here to her advice. Not all births are the result of intercourse between a man and a woman; various technologies ranging from artificial insemination to in vitro fertilization also create babies. Further, not all adoption stories are quite so rosy. Sometimes a birth mother gives up a child because he or she was conceived through rape or abuse or other circumstances that would be difficult for a young child to absorb. If these are characterized as "love," the adopted child may feel resentful later on when she or he learns more about their birth situation. Every adoption story has unique elements and circumstances that adoptive parents need to figure out how to weave together into a truthful account that can be shared with their child at different stages of the child's development. Each family must decide what information and how much to share with their child. We were told early in the adoption process that we should not lie to our children because children either know when someone is lying to them or they eventually discover the truth. We have watched as friends have damaged their relationships with their children because they did not tell the truth and their children eventually discovered the lie. We feel strongly that parents should always be truthful with their children. That said, however, parents don't need to tell their children every detail, especially when children are very young, nor do they need to add details that embellish the story. Listen closely to what your child asks you. Keep your response simple, understandable, and limited to the question you were asked.

STAGE 3—*"I'M ADOPTED!"*

The third stage of understanding occurs between ages 8 and 11, when children begin to understand the concept of blood relatives. At this stage, children often grieve for their birth parents. It's important to encourage your children at this stage to express their feelings. You can let them know that it is normal to be sad when they are thinking about their birth parents. Keeping the lines of communication open between you and your child at this stage is critical. Let your children know that it's okay to talk about their birth parents and to be curious about where they were born. At this point in their development, children are ready for answers to the questions they ask. One of our sons began to grieve for his birth mother when he was about 11 years old. We had always planned to share the information we had about their birth families with both of our sons, but we expected to do it when they were several years older. Our son was so upset, however, that we decided to ask him if he wanted to read his file. He said yes. Because he didn't have a "happy" adoption story, we were concerned that reading the file might upset him even more, but we didn't know what else might alleviate his sadness. We sat with him as he read his file and assured him that we would answer any questions he might have (although we did tell him that we might not know the answers to all of his questions). He read the file, asked a few questions, thanked us for sharing it with him, and said he felt better knowing his story. He never asked about his birth family again. When we asked our other son if he would like to read his file, he asked, "Will it take long?" Each child is different. Parents need to think ahead about how they will respond to a child's questions about his or her birth, but they also need to be flexible and willing to respond differently if necessary.

This is also a time when an adopted child needs to know that there are other adopted children, and preferably to know some other adopted children. As a child begins to understand that most of the children who live in the neighborhood or go to his or her school are related by blood to their parents, the child can begin to feel isolated, alone, and even like a freak. This can intensify if the child hears stories of someone who is trying hard to have a baby and really wants one of "their own." Having friends who are also adopted helps normalize the child's situation. One of the reasons we joined our adoption group was to ensure that our children would know (and we hoped would also become friends with) other adopted black and biracial children who were being parented by white lesbians. The likelihood that they would just naturally find other children their age who were in similar families was minimal at best. Joining the group gave them and us a set of friends who normalized our lives and anchored our children as they got older.

The family relocation to a new home that we noted at the beginning of this chapter occurred when the boys were 9 and 11. As we said, a puppy was part of our deal with the boys. Shortly after we brought the puppy home, one of our sons said, "Now we're the typical American family—two parents, two children, and a dog." Although we thought it comical that he would identify two white lesbians raising two African American boys as the "typical" American family, we were pleased that our son believed we were. He may have been a little ahead of the cultural curve when he made that comment, but with NBC's new comedy show, *The New Normal*, about gay and lesbian parents, debuting in the fall 2012 lineup, he clearly was on to something.

STAGE 4—*"WHO ARE MY BIRTH PARENTS?"*

By the time children reach adolescence (12–13 years), they understand that adoption is the legal transfer of parental rights and responsibilities. At this stage, adopted children often become more curious about their birth parents. Again, parents need to make sure that their children know that their curiosity is okay and that it's okay to talk about their birth parents. In fact, parents can even initiate discussions about birth parents. Melina concludes that, "In many respects, it is the attitude we convey to children, not the words we use, that is most important. That attitude should be open, empathetic, and honest." Melina's advice is sound, but sometimes difficult to follow, especially for white adoptive parents of children of color.

Discussions about the birth parents of children of color, particularly African American or Hispanic birth parents, often lead to complicated issues about race, ethnicity, and social class. Many African American and Hispanic children are given up for adoption by birth parents who are too poor to care for them. The parents often are also very young and uneducated, which means that they are not likely to be able to provide a stable economic future for the child. In contrast, adoptive parents, primarily because they have to meet rigorous income and housing requirements in order to be allowed by the state to legally adopt a child, tend to be middle or upper-middle class, educated, and older. They also tend to be white. Black groups, in fact, often point to the income and housing requirements for adoption as a reason why African Americans are precluded from adopting children, thus leading to the large numbers of whites who adopt black children. They say that whites are unfairly advantaged by current adoption regulations given that whites have, on average, higher incomes and more wealth than blacks. When black or Hispanic children ask their middle-class white parents about their birth parents and learn that they were most likely young, poor, and uneducated, they are receiving information that reinforces what they have begun to learn from the world around them: *Being black or Hispanic means being lower social class.* The issue is not the same for white adoptees, even if their birth parents were young, poor, and uneducated, because they do not learn from the culture that being white means being lower social class.

In talking with your child about the social and economic conditions that led his or her birth parents to choose adoption (or, in some cases, to be forced to give up their child for adoption), it's important to lay the foundation for a more complex discussion of the relationship between race and social class. Don't let assumptions about that relationship go unchallenged. A ten-year-old child may not be ready to understand a complex argument about the causes of economic disparities between blacks and whites, but he or she can be taught about the history and legacy of slavery in the U.S. and about the ways that institutional racism continues to make it difficult for blacks to accumulate wealth and move ahead economically and socially. Children of this age can understand facts. These discussions are closely tied to helping your child develop a healthy racial identity. You want your son or daughter to be proud of his or her racial identity and to understand that race and social class are not inherently or biologically connected. Being black or Hispanic does not predetermine being poor. You also don't want them to believe that they are not poor because they were adopted by white parents. In many cases adoption does give a child born to parents in difficult circumstances a better chance in life. That better chance is as likely to be true for adoptees of any race and also true regardless of the race of the adoptive parents. Non-white adoptive parents also give their adopted children a better chance in life. Children of color who are adopted by white parents need to understand that they have a good life not because their adoptive parents are white but because they are part of a loving family—and because adoptive parents, regardless of race or ethnicity, have to meet income requirements that give them economic advantages.

Questions about birth parents also raise difficult issues for parents of adoptees born in other countries. Adoptees from China, Korea, and India are more likely to be girls than boys because these cultures value boys more. A girl baby is less valuable to the birth family and the society and so is more likely to be put up for international adoption. There have been stories for many years about poor mothers in Colombia and other parts of South America who have sold their babies, sometimes willingly and sometimes forcibly, for money to support their families. These cultural narratives are painful for parents to talk about with their children, but they cannot be avoided. It's much better to talk now with your child than to be confronted later by questions from an angry or distraught child who has been learning about these cultural issues on his or her own. It's important, however, to make sure that you talk with your child in a way that avoids making cultural judgments that presume U.S. culture is superior to your child's birth culture. Current political rhetoric about American leadership in the world makes this doubly difficult. Delegates at both the Republican National Convention and Democratic National Convention in 2012 loudly chanted "USA" whenever a speaker talked about the superiority of the U.S. That message is ubiquitous in the national discourse, creating a need for adoptive parents of children born outside of the U.S. to work doubly hard to ensure that their children understand the strengths of their birth culture.

Talking about race— *"Why am I different and what does it mean?"*

White parents of children of color find themselves in a new and often disconcerting position with regard to talking about race. Although blacks talk about race often, whites are less likely to talk about it, and, in fact, often avoid the topic. As we've said several times before, whites generally don't think about themselves as having a race and, therefore, usually don't talk about race as a meaningful aspect of their everyday lives, at least not in reference to themselves. Race is something that is assigned to people of color and, therefore, talked about only in reference to people of color. Once you become the parent of a child of color, however, you lose the privilege of not thinking about race in reference to yourself and to everyday life. As a member of an interracial family, you will be identified by others as having a racial identity ("the white woman with the black kids"/"the white man with the Asian girl") and you will most likely become more racially aware as you help your child navigate through the culture and develop his or her racial identity. In talking about how to help your child develop a healthy racial identity, we've discussed ways to help your child learn about her or his cultural background. As you do these things—for example, acquire black literature, learn about black history, attend plays or films about black experiences—you can use the activities as a way to talk with your child about what you are both learning. These discussions can both deepen your shared learning and remind your child that you are open to talking about race.

How you talk about race with your child will depend on your child's age and development. Younger children, who see race as a physical characteristic, will not understand conversations about race as socially constructed or about the ways in which race and class are intertwined. They will, however, understand when you tell them that they have beautiful brown skin. What is most important is that your children understand—from the time they are very young—that you are not afraid to talk about race and that you are always willing to talk about it with them and to answer their questions as well as you can.

In addition to talking about race through your shared experiences, you can create other opportunities to talk about race. As we highlighted in Chapter 3, dinner conversations about events in the news provide many openings to discussions about race. For example, when Representative Joe Wilson of Alabama yelled "liar" during President Obama's State of the Union speech in 2009, some political commentators said his behavior was racist. Others disagreed and said it was simply disrespectful. The incident opens the door to a discussion about why Wilson's behavior could be construed as racist and why people tended to split along racial lines in their assessment of whether or not he did commit a racist act.

Sometimes your child will experience situations that will present an opportunity to talk about race. For example, when our sons were in middle school, the private school they attended hosted a performance by a hip-hop dance group from Boston that had been the recipient of a grant by a local charitable foundation. The dance troupe members were all urban boys and girls. When we arrived at the event, the parking lot was full so we dropped the boys off at the auditorium and told them to get seats for all of us while we parked the car. When we got to the auditorium, they said they had a weird experience with some community people attending the event, who stopped them and asked if they were in the dance troupe. Our sons were wearing their "special occasion" school uniforms—khaki pants, navy blazers, shirt, and tie—and they were walking into the auditorium with other people attending the event. There was no reason for anyone to assume they were in the dance troupe, other than the fact that they had black skin. A year or so later, we attended a classical music concert in the same town. Throughout the concert an older woman seated a few rows away from us stared at the boys. After the concert ended and we were leaving the theater, the woman walked over to us and asked if the boys were members of the "lost boys of Sudan," some of whom had been hosted by local families for a short time. Marlene quickly said, "No. They are my sons."

Both situations led to discussions with the boys about race and social class. In both instances, the people who assumed they knew the boys' identity were filtering their perceptions through cultural assumptions about race and social class. In the first instance, the individuals who asked the boys if they were members of the hip-hop group couldn't imagine why young black boys would be attending the event unless they had come from someplace else to perform, even though they were dressed in the uniform of the school hosting the performance. In the second instance, the woman who assumed the boys had escaped from Sudan couldn't imagine that black boys in her community could be from anywhere other than another country. The inability of these individuals to see our sons simply as young men who lived in the community spoke to cultural assumptions about blackness and social class. Black children don't attend private schools and classical music concerts. The incidents gave our family much to talk about.

White parents of Asian or Hispanic children face similar situations in which they need to talk with their children about racial stereotypes. For Asian children the stereotype is often seen as a positive characteristic, for example, Asian children are smart, exceptionally good in math, and proficient violinists and pianists. The stereotypes may not be negative, but they create internalized racism for the Asian child who doesn't do well in school generally or in math particularly. And they are always constraining for the child who prefers literature or history to math or playing basketball rather than the piano.

As we said in Chapter 3, children's understanding of race develops over time, as does their own racial identity and awareness. Very young children see race as a set of physical characteristics; older children begin to see negative stereotypes and prejudice; teens begin to develop a sense of racial and ethnic pride and also begin to express their identity through their appearance and belief system. How you talk with your child about race depends on where your child is developmentally. A four-year-old child cannot process a discussion of the relationship of race and social class. She or he can, however, absorb positive messages from you about black people: "Black people are nice, they are beautiful, they are smart. You are black. You are nice, beautiful, and smart." Most parents understand the importance of encouraging their child to have a positive self-image. Many parenting guides discuss how to teach your child positive self-regard, teachers are encouraged to tell students what they do well rather than focusing only on what they do poorly, and popular culture is rife with stories of well-known people who credit their success to a mother or father who told them they could be anything they wanted to be or do anything they wanted to do. In her 2012 speech at the Republican National Convention, former Secretary of State Condoleezza Rice, who is African American, concluded with a personal story about growing up in segregated Birmingham, Alabama where her parents convinced her that "even if she cannot have a hamburger at Woolworth's, she can be the President of the United States if she wanted to be, and she becomes the Secretary of State."

The advice to give your children positive messages about themselves is doubly important for white parents of children of color. Teaching your child positive self-regard in a world in which he or she is taught self-hatred or at least marginal status requires constant vigilance. Many white parents grew up in a world in which they believed they could accomplish anything if they worked hard and persevered. That is not to say that all white parents grew up economically advantaged. Even those who grew up poor or working class, however, lived in a world in which they could see themselves reflected in the images of successful people. In contrast, black parents have experienced racism, and they understand the need to work to keep their children from absorbing the negative attitudes and beliefs about blacks that are so dominant in the larger culture. White parents of children of color need to learn that same lesson. It's helpful to draw on personal experiences of feeling different as a child as a way to develop empathy with what your child is experiencing. Kids who have to wear glasses might at first think people are staring at them. Kids with acne often experience severe self-consciousness and doubts about their appearance. Whatever experiences you as a parent recall, remember that what you experienced for a short time or infrequently throughout your life, your child experiences every day.

Conversations with a young child can also focus on questioning the child's assumptions about what they see. If they say that a black doll isn't pretty, ask why they think that. If they don't like a book by a black author, ask why. Try to uncover misperceptions they may have. You can also say that you think the doll is pretty or explain that the book is based on real-life circumstances. Of course, only tell your child the doll is pretty if, in fact, it is. There are numerous examples of dolls of every shade that are unattractive, and there are lots of reasons not to like a particular book. So if the doll is unattractive, you can agree that it is, and if the book is not about your child's favorite subject, you can recognize that. But in either case, be sure that you make clear that the judgments should not be about the race of the doll or the author.

Other issues related to physical characteristics may come up at this time in a child's life. When our sons were in preschool, they complained that other children would come up to them and run their hands over their heads. We saw white children do this to other black children in our sons' preschool and later in elementary school, and we often heard the parents of black children comment on the behavior and say their children also didn't like it. We explained to our sons that the white children were fascinated by their hair because it looked so different and they were simply curious about how it felt. Their fascination, however, didn't give them the right to violate our sons' personal space. We explained that others shouldn't touch them without permission and that it was okay to say, "Please don't touch my hair." We also told them that they had beautiful hair. When they were young, these experiences were opportunities to reinforce the idea that people are different physically and those differences are beautiful. As the boys grew older, we used these experiences as points of reference for talking about race and the ways that people judge others based on their physical differences. The important point is to be open to and even encourage discussions about race, but to keep the discussions at the level that your child can understand. Begin with words that describe physical differences. As your child gets older, move to using names for different racial and ethnic heritages. Give them words that help them describe themselves, for example, "I am an African American (or biracial) child in an interracial (or multiracial) family." Talk about the importance of using the names people choose for themselves, and later begin to explain how the names for racial and ethnic groups often change over time in response to cultural changes.

A related conversation with your child will be about the ways in which the English language itself encourages negative comments about blacks. The actor and scholar, Ossie Davis, gave a now-famous speech to the American Federation of Teachers in 1966 in which he declared that "the English language is my enemy" (p.10). Davis examined *Roget's Thesaurus* and found 134 synonyms for whiteness, of which 44 were favorable and only 10 were unfavorable. In contrast, blackness had 120 synonyms, 60 of which were unfavorable and none of which were favorable. Speakers of English learn at a young age to equate whiteness with cleanliness, purity, and goodness and black with dirt, darkness, and evil. Davis concluded that "any teacher…who uses the English Language as a medium of communication is forced, willy-nilly, to teach the Negro child 60 ways to despise himself, and the white child 60 ways to aid and abet him in the crime" (p.12). We generally use language without thinking much about how our word choice might affect others, even when we are aware of the power of language to shape people's understanding of the world, and even to hurt others. Marlene recalls running into a colleague in the supermarket one day when the boys were with her and having a conversation about one of the offices on her campus. After referring to it as a "black hole" and realizing that the boys were listening closely, she understood for the first time how the phrase, which she used often and unthinkingly, reinforced negative images of blackness.

Our point is not that white parents need to monitor everything they say. Doing so would drive you crazy. But understanding that language can be damaging to your child's identity is important, both in helping you use language more carefully and in talking about language with your child. Recognizing how difficult it is for you to monitor your language offers a glimpse into the difficulties facing your child in using English every day.

One conversation that black families have with their sons that white parents of black children need to have also is "The Talk." Similar to the conversation we described in Chapter 2 in which parents discuss DWB ("driving while black"), "The Talk" prepares young black men for how to deal with the cultural perception of black men as violent and threatening. Black males are more likely to be stopped by the police when they are driving, shadowed by security when they are shopping, and identified as perpetrators of crimes by witnesses than are men of other races. In a media saturated culture, the barrage of negative images of black males often results in fear that any black male might be violent and dangerous. One black father said it was better to have "The Talk" than face the possibility of burying his son (Bowman 2012). Talking about race may be hard for whites, but learning how to do it is imperative for white parents of black children. Your children may not accept the content of "The Talk" but they will hear it, which is important.

This brings us to a more general point and one final piece of advice as we end this chapter. If you are talking with your child about race and/or adoption and your child doesn't respond, don't assume your son or daughter is not listening to you. Conversations that are difficult for you are probably also difficult for your child. This is the case with all sensitive subjects—sexual behavior, drugs, alcohol, violence. Children (and adults) need time to process conversations about adoption and race, just as they need time to process conversations about other difficult topics. These topics are complex and rife with emotions. Your child may appear to be blowing you off today, but will benefit from what she or he has heard tomorrow.

Things to consider

- *Racism takes many forms, sometimes intentional but often unintentional, and you need to help your child understand this.* White parents of adopted children of color must learn to recognize racism in all of its forms—interpersonal, institutional, and internalized—in order to help your child deal with it.

- *Race and social class are intertwined in U.S. culture.* Many people assume a person of color must be poor and of lower social class. This assumption may affect how people treat your child, and you should be prepared to talk frankly about this.

- *A child's understanding of adoption develops over time.* Be open and honest in talking with your child about her or his adoption, but use language and provide details that are appropriate to your child's age. Answer the questions you are asked.

- *Provide your child with his or her adoption story.* An adoption story gives your child a sense of belonging and place within your family and gives both of you a shared experience that you can then share with others.

- *Recognize that "race matters."* Talk about race and encourage your child to talk about it and share his or her experiences as a child of color. Check in with your child about those experiences.

- *Let your child know that you are always open to talking about race and adoption, even when the issues are difficult or painful.* Whether the subject is your child's birth parents, a racist comment made by a teacher, or why so many black people are poor, let your child know that you are willing to talk about it.

References

Bowman, B.B. (2012) "Black families address racism with 'The Talk'." *Medill Reports*. 8 May. Available at http://news.medill.northwestern.edu/chicago/news.aspx?id+205251, accessed on 7 February 2013.

Davis, O. (1966) "The English Language is My Enemy." In O. Davis (2006) *Life Lit By Some Large Vision: Selected Speeches and Writings*. New York: Atria Books.

"Dear Margo." (2012) *The Boston Globe*, 13 November, p.G23.

Henry, M.J. and Pollack, D. (2009) *Adoption in the United States*. Chicago, IL: Lyceum Books.

Melina, L. (2003) "Adoption Through a Child's Eyes." *Adoptive Families*. Available at www.adoptivefamilies.com/articles/643/age-by-age-talking-to-kids-about-adoption, accessed on 7 February 2013.

Rice, C. (2012) "Transcript of Condoleezza Rice speech at the RNC." 20 August. Available at www.foxnews.com/politics/2012/08/29/transcript-condoleezza-rice-speech-at-rnc, accessed on 7 February 2013.

Siegel, D.H. and Smith, S.L. (2012) "Openness in Adoption: From Secrecy and Stigma to Knowledge and Connections." Evan B. Donaldson Adoption Institute. Available at www.adoptioninstitute.org/research/2012_03_openness.php, accessed on 7 February 2013.

Tompkins, S. (2011) "Let's Play Adoption." *Adoptive Families*. Available at www.adoptivefamilies.com/articles/199/, accessed on 23 July 2012.

Resources

Callahan, N. M. (2011) "Talking to your child about adoption: Recommendations for parents." *Adoption Advocate*, 42, 1–6. Available at *www.adoptioncouncil.org/publications/adoption-advocate-no-42.html.*

This article provides valuable tips about talking to your children about adoption—be they adopted as infants or as older children, either domestically or internationally. The article includes advice on helping your child talk with others about being adopted.

Keefer, B. and Schooler, J.E. (2000) *Telling the Truth to Your Adopted or Foster Child—Making Sense of the Past*. Westport, CT: Bergin & Garvey.

We found this book especially valuable when we were at the stage of talking with our sons about adoption. Chapters 7–10 provide excellent overviews and advice about parent–child communication, with Chapter 10 dealing explicitly with transracial and transcultural adoption.

Wilkerson, I. (2010) *The Warmth of Other Suns: The Epic Story of America's Great Migration*. New York: Random House.

This award-winning book provides a detailed and moving account of the migration of six million blacks in the U.S. from World War I through the 1970s who left the South and headed to northern and western cities in search of a better life.

CHAPTER 5

Navigating School—
Homework for Parents

All white adoptive parents of children of color face an avalanche of questions, decisions, uncertainties, second guesses, and surprises when their children enter school. Day care and preschool provide a rehearsal for what is to come, but the stakes quickly increase when the formal school process begins. We were shocked, for example, when we learned that our town did not have full-day kindergarten. That meant a separate after-school program or private kindergarten. We had certainly thought about issues of race and diversity when our children were in day care and preschool, but we knew that our family was now entering a long process of curriculum, grading, peer groups, and parent involvement in school. And then came the gut-wrenching questions: how will those entrusted with our child handle the adoption issue? What attitudes about race and interracial adoption will our family encounter? For those who adopt older children, all these concerns are present plus added worries about adjustment and, for most children adopted from outside the U.S., legitimate concerns about both the child's learning English and maintaining his or her native language. All adoptive parents have to confront the ways in which school projects and curriculum take for granted that the child's parents are biological. If you have adopted a child of color, another layer is added to every dimension of schooling and decision-making about what's best for your child. What's better or worse? What can we settle for? What issues involve race, might involve race, probably do not involve race but then again...? What are the implications of getting it wrong? Or of assuming too much about the good intentions of others? From elementary school forward, one-third of a child's life occurs in the school context, onto which are added school-related activities, social activities, and contacts that originate in school.

In this chapter, we discuss four key school-related issues that adoptive parents of black and other children of color face: (1) decisions about where your child should attend school and factors associated with school location; (2) ensuring appropriate expectations for your child; (3) strategies when you suspect your child is being treated unfairly because of race; and (4) the role of parents in creating greater awareness of diversity issues in the school setting. Some of the issues are exactly the same for children of color generally, while others are unique to black children but may suggest useful comparisons. In considering the racial matrix for children of color who are adopted by white parents, a complex set of relations exists among the child, the parent, the community, and the school.

- What decisions do parents need to make about where they live, where their children attend school, and how both factors impact the communities that will be central to them and their children?

- How do white parents talk with black parents and other white parents as they deal with issues of race and schooling?

- How do white parents talk with their adopted black children about race in the context of school?

- How do white parents handle comments their adopted black children make about racial incidents at school and how race is handled in the curriculum and out-of-class activities and interactions?

- How do white parents of adopted black children intervene when they think race has been dealt with inappropriately in their adopted black child's educational experience or at school in general?

White parents are at a disadvantage in preparing for the many racial challenges that will arise for their black adopted children in the process of their education. Snyder recently reported on an interview study in which she was interested in "how multiracial people of African descent experience racism in schools and…how their parents or guardians prepare them to cope with incidents of racism in school" (Synder 2012, p.228). She compared those with white parents to those with at least one black parent, concluding that those with white parents were less effectively socialized to deal with racism and less likely to talk about race with their parents than those with at least one black parent. These results make sense intuitively and point to the necessity for white parents of black children to be keenly attentive to issues of race in their children's schooling, meaning that a steep learning curve will be necessary. That steep learning curve will be encountered over and over as your child moves through the school years.

Deciding on schools—*Location, location, location*

We begin with a caveat. For some parents, decisions about where your child will be attending school are not flexible. This may be the case because of financial resources, work constraints, family or personal issues, care arrangements for younger children, after-school programs, or other factors. In these cases, all of the other considerations discussed here that bear on your child's race and her or his multiracial family will still be relevant. It may turn out that you are essentially "stuck" in a school system not of your choosing, making all the other school issues even more pressing.

As prospective white parents of black children, we were advised by black friends that quality of educational experience should trump all other considerations when making decisions about schools for our children. We understood the logic of this advice but also knew that as white parents of black children, we would face stiff challenges. In Massachusetts, our state of residence, taking that advice would mean a balancing act between school quality and diversity of community and student body. Suddenly the variables involved in our choosing where to live became much more complicated. Finding both diversity and educational quality is often impossible, which is a major outcome of the coupling of race and social class in our society (see Chapter 3) and more generally of institutional racism (see Chapter 1).

For us, as with many parents, the context for thinking about schools included where we would be living, how much commuting time to and from work would be involved for both of us, diversity in the community, diversity among students, teachers, and staff, and feedback about the schools from others we knew and with whom we could be in contact through networking. For some parents, choosing a public or private school also figures in the mix.

Neighborhood and community in early childhood education

The decision to adopt a child of color magnifies the importance of where to live and why. All prospective parents will likely be thinking about where they currently live and whether or not it's suitable for raising a family: is our house large enough? is the neighborhood safe? are there recreation areas close by?

White adoptive parents of children of color will have additional questions. Neighborhoods and schools now need to be scrutinized for how your multiracial family—meaning white parents and children of color—will fit in, how others will respond to you, and the likelihood that the community will be welcoming. Once we had determined that we would be adopting black children, we tried to approach these questions "rationally" but also had flashes of fear that someone might spray paint racist graffiti on our house or taunt our children while they were out riding their bikes. It's impossible to predict exactly how location will matter over the longer term, but you can figure out what experiences your family is likely to encounter in a particular community.

In many families, day care and preschool choices are tied to cost, how time can be juggled to accommodate drop-off and pick-up, the certainty that there will be days when your child is ill, and so forth. Some people have day care choices at work, which helps. But for adopted children and children of color, race and ethnicity present additional factors to be considered. Although adoptive parents are encouraged to begin talking to their children about adoption when they are toddlers and preschool age, children at this age, even though they can identify themselves as adopted, have little understanding of what that means (Fishman and Harrington 2007). Add racial differences between the child and his or her parents, and the complexity may be beyond the child's ability to understand—except for concrete recognition that the child looks different from his or her parents and that other families look different from their family. What is critical from the parents' perspective is vigilance about how day care providers and preschool teachers handle the concrete questions about appearance, especially hair and skin color. As we noted in Chapter 4, some of the white children in preschool wanted to touch our sons' hair because it was "different." It was important for the teacher to set boundaries for the children's contact with one another, yet not deny differences in appearance or suggest that black, nappy hair was bad or undesirable.

The importance of research

By the time a child is approaching kindergarten, parents tend to be more concerned about what's best *based on race as one major factor*. You will want to ask where specific racial and ethnic groups live. Are they concentrated in one area or dispersed throughout the community? Once you know the answer for a community, then you will want to seek out as much information as possible for those school districts that seem like good possibilities. We cannot stress enough the importance of doing thorough research and understanding what your results mean. It's important to look at community demographics, not just overall but by age group. If you are likely to adopt a child of elementary school age, be ready to ask about the demographics for that age group. Also look at a broad range of school data, including student performance on state examinations, high school graduation rates, and what students do following high school graduation. One of the most important statistics to know is the percentage of graduating seniors who go on to four-year colleges, which provides a quick reference to both the academic orientation of the schools and the community norms and aspirations for young people. Fortunately, many data sources are available on the internet. The challenge is to sort through what you find. The research alone is not, of course, the answer to where your child should attend school or how your child will fare in that school.

In large metropolitan areas, most of the "best schools" as measured by standardized test scores, quality of the colleges attended by graduates, and expenditure per pupil are located in the suburbs. The students are predominantly white, and black students are scarcely present. Suppose you are considering two different school districts. District A has 18 percent minority students (5% black, 9% Hispanic, 3% Asian, and 1% other); 71 percent of high school graduates go on to attend four-year colleges. District B has 6 percent minority students (2% black, 1% Hispanic, 2+% Asian, and a few others); 94 percent of high school graduates go on to attend four-year colleges. A is more diverse, but B seems to prepare students better for college. The best course of action would be to dig deeper for information about both districts. How are the black students distributed by grade level? In District A, what Asian backgrounds are represented? For District B, good advice would be to seek out the parents of the black children (there will not be many) and talk with them if possible. In the abstract, there is no right or wrong choice, because each family will have different priorities. For us personally, quality of schools was more important than diversity, but we know others who decided differently. In some metropolitan areas, there are communities that are both racially and economically diverse, and many adoptive parents of children of color find these to be good choices. School choice may also be an option that opens up possibilities.

Charter schools and magnet schools present another public school option in many locales—mainly urban. The jury on charter schools is still out, but depending on where a family with white parents and black adopted children lives, these schools might provide a good option. Many charter schools enroll more children of color than traditional public schools. The better ones will have waiting lists or a lottery for an enrollment spot. Although charter schools may be a good choice for some families, they are not for others. For example, charter schools typically provide fewer services for special education students beyond what is mandated by law.

The private school option

Some adoptive parents will be making decisions between public and private schools. Overall, about 10 percent of school age children attend private schools. In 2009–2010, 39 percent of private school attendees were in Catholic schools, 38 percent in other religiously-affiliated schools, and 23 percent in independent schools (National Center for Education Statistics

2012). Most independent schools require entrance tests and interviews, with the most selective ones handling admissions similarly to colleges and universities.

Some parents choose to send their adopted children of color to private schools for elementary grades, shifting to public schools later on. One advantage is that most private schools have lower student–faculty ratios, greater flexibility in curriculum, and ample arts and sports programs. Many also focus more intensively on diversity and multicultural education in the curriculum. For the junior high school/middle-school years, some privates provide a better environment for dealing with critical maturational issues that come with adolescence, such as gender relations, sex education, and bullying.

Although tuition at most independent private schools is prohibitive for many parents, more private schools now offer financial assistance. Once the domain of the white upper-middle and upper economic classes, students who attend many independent privates today represent greater economic and racial/ethnic diversity. In fact, where we live, some private schools have greater racial/ethnic diversity than public schools in the same community. There are no data on the number of adopted children in private schools, but when issues of race are involved, it's likely that at least some sector of white parents who adopt children of color will be considering the private school option. Our network of adoptive families includes every combination from all public school, to mixed public and private, to all private.

In addition to cost, when evaluating a private school, you should consider the racial and economic mix of students, the school's approach to teaching and learning styles, its proximity to home and to your workplaces, and the reputation of the school. These factors shift over time in unexpected ways. Our sons, for example, attended private school from kindergarten through the 8th grade. They started in a Montessori school that was close to home and had some diversity among the children.

Later, they shifted to a more traditional school that was an hour away from our home and not on the way to work for either of us. We managed initially, but when it was clear that school activities would be increasing as the children moved to higher grades and that it would be difficult to arrange for social interactions with school friends outside of school, we made the difficult decision to move. In choosing our new location, the main factors were proximity to the children's school, decreasing our commute time, and the option that the boys could attend a public high school that met most of our criteria. We know other families who made the decision about where to live before their children started school and then worked around that home location as they dealt with school choice issues. We also know parents who made decisions to go for a racially diverse school in the lower grades but then shifted to a more conventional, less diverse school that offered better academic preparation.

Scarcity of teachers of color

For all types of schools, the presence of teachers of color continues to be a substantial challenge. In 2011, 84 percent of public school teachers were white; 7 percent were black, and 6 percent Hispanic (Feistritzer 2011). The main culprit lies with the education profession, where work-life earnings for education majors are the lowest over the professional lifespan of all occupations (Julian 2012). Teacher "burn out" is another problem. Teaching is a high intensity job day in and day out, and many young teachers—regardless of their race—leave for other career options after a few years.

The delicate balance in simply being different

Regardless of the school, families with white parents and adopted children of color will be perceived as "different." That means that you and your child will experience the school and its related activities in ways that will depart significantly from the experience of racially-matched families. Our experience, for example, was that some black families welcomed us, while others seemed suspicious of us. Some welcomed our children into their homes for social occasions, but excluded us from their social activities. Some black parents of black children may seem to have no reservations about their children visiting your home, and others might refuse to allow their children to visit. A new set of dynamics occurs when black children with white parents reach the age of dating and romantic relationships. The parents of a black female may be pleased when they see that her boyfriend is black, but less so when they learn that his parents are white.

As children grow, peers and peer culture displace much of what parents try to instill in their children. The schools that children attend are not only the key to their educational experience but also to their friendships, first romantic relationships, and sense of identity in the peer group. Parents have little control over how these factors develop once the child reaches adolescence. If one-third of your child's life is lived in school, even more is experienced through peer culture. Prospective white parents of adopted children of color need to balance planning about school with flexibility in adapting to what occurs once your child moves through the schooling process.

Academic achievement—*Great expectations or…good enough*

White friends, when their adopted black child was in kindergarten, were surprised to learn at their first parent conference that their child was not performing especially well on basic tasks. The white teacher reported that the child was well-behaved, demonstrated social skills appropriate to his age, and was well-liked by his peers. The teacher did not seem overly concerned about the relatively lower level of skills compared to the norms she reported for kindergarten. Our friends were surprised both because they had no indication from the teacher prior to the conference of any difficulties and because they did not see their son's behavior at home as consistent with this early academic evaluation. What was going on? Perhaps the child was, indeed, not meeting skill levels in school. Perhaps the teacher had provided extra assistance to boost the child's skill levels. But perhaps not. Perhaps the teacher felt sorry for the child and thought he was doing "good enough" given the circumstances. This is one of those instances where the race of the child matters tremendously because of the long history of lower expectations for black children (Landsman 2004).

We've previously noted the ways in which school curriculum and teacher expectations linger as sources of *institutional racism*. White parents who adopt black children will necessarily be concerned that the educational experience maximizes their children's potential, but also that the expectations are appropriate to their children and not influenced by their race and gender. Parents naturally have great expectations for their children. Regardless of a child's intelligence level, health problems, or diagnosed learning disabilities, parents expect that their child will be challenged to achieve her or his very best in school. For a complex set of reasons deeply embedded in history, media images, news reporting, and racial stereotypes, black as well as Hispanic children will often be held to a lower standard than white children. The state of Virginia, for example, recently formalized lower expectations for Latino/a and black students by setting passing test scores lower for these groups than for white students (Sanchez 2012).

Substantial research literature exists on the intertwined topics of African American students' lower achievement levels and the lower expectation levels that teachers have for African American students, especially boys. In her book, *A White Teacher Talks about Race*, Julie Landsman recounts, "Principals have told me about teachers who say openly that black boys are impossible to work with because they are hyperactive and uncontrollable. These same teachers ignore the behavior of white boys who act out" (Landsman 2009, p.28). If there is an expectation that black boys will be hyperactive and hard to control, then staying on task may be overly rewarded. And if a black boy does not conform at all to these stereotypes, then a teacher may simply be pleased with any level of consistent skills performance. Similarly, a Latino boy may be *over-rewarded* for academic performance that is only adequate simply because of the expectation that Hispanic students are less likely to graduate than non-Hispanics.

In our experience, the "you're so lucky" perception of the adopted African American child seems to spill over to the school environment in ways that can be interpreted as benign institutional racism. Especially in predominantly white suburban schools, teachers will often see the black student as "exceptional." If the student is adopted, rather than the biological child of black parents, we think it's likely that teachers carry with them the assumption that the child has been lifted up from bad circumstances and therefore cannot be expected to be on a par with her or his white peers. If your black child is relatively well-behaved and polite, everything the child does that shows compliance and work at grade level will be seen as "good enough." There is no way to confirm this pattern, but our experience and what we've heard from others tell us it's there. Adoptive parents of black children should at least be aware. Expectations provide powerful motivators for all children and should be appropriate for the child's abilities and learning style.

Adoptive white parents of black and Latino/a children must always be alert to any indication that the teacher or other school personnel is "amazed" by your child's performance. If you suspect that your child is held to lower expectations than seem appropriate to you, contact the teacher to set up a time to meet or at least talk by phone. If the interaction is unsatisfactory, go to a higher level—perhaps an administrator or guidance counselor.

We recall a dinner conversation we had at a white friend's home when our children were still toddlers. One of the other guests recounted being told by Louise Lazare, who with her husband Aaron had adopted eight children of various racial backgrounds, that of all the issues she had anticipated as the white mother of children of color, the one that shocked her most was that many teachers had lower expectations for her children than she thought justified.

Responding to unfair treatment because of race—*"Tenisha, what's your view as a black person?"*

As college professors at institutions where students of color are in the minority, we have become sensitized to various classroom practices that have racial overtones and might be perceived as racist by students of color (and some white students). In a class discussion about race and ethnicity, teachers will often try to solicit as many viewpoints as possible, sometimes asking the single student of color in the room what he or she thinks about the issue—What do blacks think about this? What do Hispanics think about this? Although best practices in classroom teaching *at all levels* caution against singling out a student of color in a classroom that is majority white, our black college students and our sons report that some professors will focus on them to "speak for their race" or to share their experiences as members of their race. If this is an issue in the college classroom, it's certainly an issue in k-12 education also.

Spotlighting and erasure

Spotlighting, a concept drawn from the work of bell hooks (she doesn't use capital letters in her name), occurs when students are "positioned by White teachers and White peers as native informants…and cast in the role of racial spokesperson" (Carter 2008, p.232). The name refers to the practice of shining a bright light on a deer or other animal, with the effect of freezing the animal in its tracks. Conversely, black students can be ignored and erased in classroom practices that make them feel invisible. *Erasure* makes a person invisible (Irvine and Gal 1999) and in this case removes his or her distinctiveness as a person of color. Perhaps a white teacher never calls on either of the two black students in a class because he thinks he will be singling them out. Worse yet, the white teacher may simply ignore the student of color because of her or his difference or because the student makes the teacher feel awkward and self-conscious. Either way—spotlighting or erasure—the impact on the black pupil can be negative.

Black parents will be familiar with both ends of the spotlighting–erasure continuum, but most white parents will only know about this if they have been explicitly educated regarding the practice. This makes it important for white parents of children of color to explicitly ask their children to talk about race and school, never assuming that if something comes up involving race, their child will freely tell them. Even explicit probes may not always work. Marlene, who is Jewish, recalls an incident in elementary school when she was taunted by anti-Semitic comments, cried about it when she got home from school, but responded to her Jewish mother's question about what was wrong, with "nothing." Young children may be able to report incidents with what seem to be factual information, for instance, saying that a [white] child asked if her mother was a slave. Children in the middle-school years may be able to articulate how they experience the classroom. If parents know that their daughter or son has been spotlighted or ignored, it's important for them to deal directly with the teacher of the classroom involved. Sometimes teachers will mention in a parent–teacher conference that there have been instances where white students spotlighted a black student. In either case, probing how the teacher responded or will respond in the future can be important to how the teacher handles the classroom. Seeking advice from others, including other parents, teachers you know, and even older students can yield helpful tips on how to proceed with the teacher, or if necessary, with school administrators.

Problems with school assignments and assumptions

Standard school assignments can pose challenging and uncomfortable experiences for adopted children, regardless of their race. The "family tree" assignment is notoriously problematic for adoptive families. Children in elementary school will often be asked to create simple family trees or other representations of their families. Older children receive more complex assignments that require research on family history. The first question you and your child must deal with is "what family tree?" The metaphor of the tree implies roots and the flow of blood lines, making the assignment feel exclusionary for an adopted child. Our boys attended a small private middle school for boys where every student was expected to present his family tree at an evening celebration for students in his grade and their parents, other family members, and friends. Both boys used the project to talk about being adopted and to learn about their racial and ethnic history. Our older son explored the connection between Marlene's family being unable to trace their history because most members died in the Holocaust and his birth family's inability to trace their history because they were most likely slaves. This was part of his project, which was complemented by a detailed family tree that taught him about the two sides of his adoptive parents' families. Our younger son used the assignment to explore the slave routes from Africa to the U.S. and to speculate on his birth family's history. In his project, there was little that looked like the standard family tree. In its place were illustrations of how slaves were packed into boats and copies of slave ledgers in which slave owners listed information about the slaves they owned. In both cases, the presentations were "exceptions" to how the assignment was completed. Except for our immediate family, there were fewer photos and more question marks. In the future, all the possibilities that now exist for tracing ancestry through historical records of the slave trade and the Human Genome Project will add new dimensions to family-centered school projects. Assignments and time-honored traditions such as the high school graduation photo display that involve baby pictures can also put an adopted child who was not adopted as an infant in a difficult position. Teachers often are unaware of how these assignments affect adopted children, requiring parents to be especially supportive in helping the child deal with the situation and coming up with ways to participate.

As we noted in Chapter 2, parents will often discover that the curriculum is limited in presenting the history of race and ethnicity in our country and the world as well as in representations of people of color. When this occurs, it's important to learn how the curriculum is set and what options are available to individual teachers. Sometimes a teacher will be able to respond directly to a suggestion, for example, of a black or Latina poet to include in the poetry unit. Sometimes you will be able to be helpful to a teacher through your suggestions, which the teacher can then take to whomever is responsible for curricular decisions. As with other issues related to race, keeping an eye on not just *what* is included but *how* race is handled in the curriculum is important. A delicate balance exists in emphasizing and calling attention to the contributions of African Americans and other people of color and simply normalizing them by including them in the curriculum. A similar point can be made about students. For history assignments, do teachers always suggest that your black daughter or son do a project on an important African American? This may be a good idea, but white students should also be encouraged to learn about the contributions of people of color. To take another example, given that few students know much at all about history, does a teacher assume too much about what your son or daughter knows about African American history, Chinese American history, etc.? Even asking a black student to comment about slavery may put that student in a difficult position, not only because of spotlighting, but also because the teacher may assume too much about what the child knows and, thus, embarrass the child. In fairness to educators, many teachers and school curricula do explicitly pay attention to inclusiveness. Like any other aspect of society, however, both institutional racism and the weight of tradition will often replicate racially unfair patterns.

Discussions with teachers also pose decision points for white parents of adopted children of color. If you, as a parent, are concerned that your son or daughter is having difficulty in school, you will likely want to talk with his or her teacher. In those conversations, however, you will often be wondering if the teacher is responding to what you have to say about your *child* or about your *black* or *Latino/a child*. Will the teacher and should the teacher perceive and filter the conversation differently because of the child's race? We are not suggesting that a parent should avoid talking with a teacher about a child's school performance simply because of potential racial perceptions. We are pointing out that trying to anticipate how a teacher may be responding and listening carefully will be important in shaping both what is said and how the parent follows through over time. This brings to mind a conversation with a black friend who was concerned about her biological son's aggressive behavior. Her inclination was to talk to his teacher both to get her perspective and to develop strategies for dealing with instances of aggressive actions. Our friend hesitated about talking to the teacher, however, because she feared that the teacher might stereotype her son as "an aggressive black boy" rather than seeing him as an individual child. The point is that there is no clear answer for how to proceed, but there is good reason to consult with others and, once contact has been made, to follow through.

School activities and frank conversations

There will be other contexts at school where a child of color will be treated unfairly. These often involve sports and other out-of-class activities. For sports, racial stereotypes emerge at all levels from elementary school through high school. If you have a black son or daughter who grows tall during adolescence, he or she is likely to be pegged as a basketball player and strongly encouraged to be on the basketball team. Broad shoulders and a muscular build on a young black boy may lead to the expectation that he will play football—regardless of his interests. It's important to listen to your children and to make it clear to them that you will support what they want to do rather than what a coach or teacher expects them to pursue. Beyond that, pointing out the patterns that have existed in society to produce an imbalance of African Americans in sports compared to other fields will be as much a parent's responsibility as a teacher's.

School activities can also present unfair situations for your child. One of our sons played in the high school band. When the band was organizing a trip to the high school's sister school in Japan, students were given the option of staying in homes or in a hostel with the chaperons. Our son, like most students, elected the home-stay option, but he was not placed. We knew about issues in Japan with racial discrimination and the stereotyping of blacks, but it didn't occur to us that a Japanese family might be reluctant to house a black male teenager. When we approached the band director, he claimed that he knew nothing about this or the reason that our son did not get a home-stay placement. He said, "It could be anything" and pushed us off to a staff member, who said he'd "try to do something." Nothing was done, and we had a good idea why not: no one wanted to confront the situation. On the positive side, our son's best male friend, who is white, opted to withdraw from his in-home assignment and stay in the hostel with our son. We also told many other parents about the situation, all of whom were supportive. In addition, our son was now forewarned that once in Japan, he might be viewed "differently" from the white students in the band. Indeed, when he returned, he reported being stared at, but at least he was prepared.

Lack of experience is a shortcoming for white parents of black children of color in situations where we think our child has been treated unfairly because of race. White parents, carrying their white privilege, sometimes underreact and sometimes overreact. We might fail to act because we do not see instances where race leads to unfair treatment. We also might not know what questions to ask our children or what conversations need to occur regularly in order for us to know what is happening in school that involves race. We might overact out of hyper-vigilance and suspicion, over-protectiveness, and guilt. Understandably most white parents of black children want to be especially careful to watch out for racially-laced events. In doing so, it's easy to project a racial or racist interpretation onto an event or situation. We were once concerned, for example, that our son never had a solo in the middle-school jazz band when all of the other trumpeters had a turn at this. We were about to approach the band teacher when we asked our son about it. He replied that he'd been asked and encouraged but didn't want to do it.

There is no right or wrong way for parents to approach situations where they suspect racism. We can only say that it would never be right to let everything slide nor to pounce on every little incident. It will always be important to respond in some way to any incidents reported by your children that they think are racist or if they think they were singled out because of their race. Parents are role models for their children, making it imperative to respond in appropriate ways to events, comments, and patterns of behavior that appear racist. Like many other challenges we discuss in this book, it's helpful to have conversations with black friends (especially those with children) and with other adoptive parents of black children.

What should parents do to help schools and teachers?—*Stepping in and staying out*

When one of our children was in the first grade at a local Montessori school, the teacher invited parents who had expertise in some area that might be meaningful to the children to propose a short lesson. Fern, who studies language and culture, thought that the children might be interested in learning that some words in American English can be traced to the African languages of the slaves. The lesson was simple and straightforward. We looked at maps of where slaves came from across the Atlantic, we imagined what it might be like to "invent" a language out of what you had spoken from birth and what was all around you as "foreign," and we talked about some words we now use that came "all the way from Africa" with the slaves: *banana, banjo, jazz, jiffy, yam, zombie.* The children enjoyed the lesson, thought the maps were cool, and had great ideas about inventing a new language. Our son also seemed to like it that his mom, who was a college teacher, knew this stuff. This suggested to both of us that it would be important to step in when possible to offer our own expertise for presentations or consultations. We knew many others who we also thought would be excellent resource people. Good idea? Well, not so fast. Sometimes offering help and relevant expertise can be good, but there are cautions too. We learned quickly that children do not necessarily want their parents at school because it's embarrassing and puts them in the spotlight. Teachers too might be sensitive about parent intrusions. Yet, white parents of adopted children of color have a role in the educational system, simply because we are not yet at the point where cultural and racial diversity are amply reflected in the curriculum or school practices.

Best practices in education suggest that teachers at any level should be willing to share the curriculum they are teaching. Most schools have parent orientations in which overviews are provided. It's important for white parents of children of color to introduce themselves to teachers and to let the teachers know the relevant circumstances for their child. This not only helps preclude embarrassment on the part of the teacher and awkward situations for the student but can also stimulate a teacher's thinking about choices they may be able to make about class discussion topics and methods and how to teach various subjects.

Parents also have a right to intercede by stepping in when problematic assignments such as the family tree or a display of baby photos place their adopted children in a stressful and awkward situation. Fishman and Harrington (2007) suggest, for example, that the family tree might be replaced by a "family forest" with many different branches and roots. We think that for African American adoptees especially, the extended family of "adopted" black relatives constitutes an important part of this forest. If a parent discovers that not only are there few black figures of importance presented in the curriculum but also that there are no black women, pointing this out to the teacher would be important. Even though many teachers will be receptive to suggestions, it's realistic to expect awkwardness or even some tension in some cases. Most teachers are white. For good or bad, white teachers may be more easily receptive to suggestions about race in the curriculum from a white parent than they would from a black parent—simply because the interaction will trigger fewer guilt feelings. At the same time, it's important for white parents of black children to be allies with black parents who raise questions about curriculum or broader matters related to the school.

There are also times for parents to play a role behind the scenes in helping create a more positive climate in school for adopted children in general and for adopted children of color more specifically. A parent might suggest someone to give a presentation on the changing American family including single parent families, blended families, multiracial families, families created through adoption, extended families, and family patterns and values that are typical for groups whose ancestry is Chinese, Mexican, Korean, Iranian, and so forth. Although adoption impacts only a small percentage of school age children, the "stick out-ness" factor can be minimized when put into the context of the multitude of family patterns now present in the United States.

Often, systemic problems in school structure, organization, and curriculum underlie problematic situations that arise related to children of color or children who are in other ways different from the mainstream. If a school district has little diversity, the student who is "different" may be treated as exotic, even if the intentions are good. We heard teachers comment many times that it was great to have a black student in the class, but we were always a little uncomfortable in thinking about what that might mean day-to-day for our child. If a child's native language is Chinese or Spanish, that alone—regardless of whether the child is adopted or not—will identify that child as "foreign" simply because the U.S. still considers all languages other than English as foreign. Many issues that specifically impact students of color also impact the entire school population. If, for example, students are not adequately prepared throughout their education to work with and understand diverse populations, they will be at a disadvantage as they pursue their vocational and professional goals. When to speak up is always a balancing act, but there will be opportunities throughout your child's education to play a role as a parent in bringing taken-for-granted assumptions into more conscious awareness for teachers and school administrators. Often these interventions will not only benefit your child but will have a positive impact on the educational process—the proverbial "a rising tide carries all boats" phenomenon.

In writing about the problem of low expectations for black students, especially boys, Landsman (2004) provides a list of questions that need to be asked of and by all schools to ensure that there are high expectations for *all* students. Among these, she urges answers to these questions:

- "Are examples of the achievements and ideas of diverse authors, thinkers, and historical figures woven into—not separated from—the curriculum?"

- "Are texts, lessons, and discussion topics chosen with thought about how to provide a safe environment for discussion of controversial issues?"

- "Does the school challenge anyone making generalizations about racial and ethnic groups?"

- "Does the school take students' and parents' discomfort, frustration, or anger seriously? Are issues worked out through mediation and discussion?"

- "Do teachers and staff members feel they can openly discuss issues of race, class, and gender without feeling defensive or ashamed?"

We would add to her list, "Does the school ask white teachers and staff members, rather than only teachers and staff of color, to deal with racial and ethnic problems that arise?"

Students who are perceived as "different" are also often subject to bullying and taunting, a subject that has received substantial attention in recent years. Children are the victims and perpetrators of bullying for many different reasons, and parents of an adopted child (especially an adopted child of color) will always need to be alert to signs that their child is stressed at school or is avoiding contact with peers. Likewise, parents cannot rule out that their child is a bully just because she or he is adopted or not white. Any parent who suspects bullying needs to report this and talk with appropriate school personnel and other parents.

Parents have a role to play in the overall educational climate of the schools their children attend, and also in intervening to deal with concrete situations affecting their child. Yet, like other challenges we have discussed, there is always a balance between intervention and pausing, and there are always choices about which battles to fight and when to fight them.

Lots of questions but more than one answer

In this chapter, we've provided a preliminary analysis of what to expect as a white parent of adopted children who are of another racial or ethnic heritage. Every adult likely remembers times at school that were stressful and lonely, and feeling helpless and discouraged. The middle-school years often bring back the worst of our memories, as we tried to adjust to personal identity development, our awkward growing bodies and sexual awareness, and the enormous pressures to fit in and be part of a group. Some adults may look back and wish their parents had been more helpful, while others wish they would have stayed out of their lives. All of these memories need to be placed into the context of what you might expect as a parent of children who are not only adopted but recognizable as racially different from you. We've highlighted the importance of understanding that black children and all children of color do not experience school in the same way as do their white peers. There's no right answer to the question of where to live, but asking the question will start in motion a more heightened awareness of a host of considerations that are important to being aware of how race, ethnicity, and adoption will impact a child's education experience. In thinking about whether to expect that teachers and other school personnel will have unjustifiable, lower standards for your black child, or higher standards for your Chinese child, the simple answer is "yes." The challenge arises in figuring out how to respond when you suspect that race is shaping how your child is perceived and judged.

  Racism continues to exist, and schools are not exempt. Anyone who says otherwise is uninformed, sheltered, or a bigot.

The consequences for slippage in the education system that result in a child not striving for or achieving what is possible for him or her far outweigh any single incident or summary of experiences. When the slippage results from racial or ethnic factors, everyone pays in multiple ways. Isolated parenting is probably never the best approach, but it is definitely not a viable approach when the children involved carry with them the history of race, along with the family circumstance of adoption.

As white parents, we have an additional responsibility because we need to learn the codes of racial thinking that we have not been aware of, and we have to take action in situations where in the past we were not looked to for assertiveness. All of us need help along the way. It may sound trite to say that "it takes a village," but there is no other option. The enormous consequences of education for a person's whole life demand that we seek advice, enter zones of discomfort, and build alliances both within the adoption community and across race outside the adoption community. We cannot think of a parent of a black child—whether that parent is black, white, or biracial—who has not encountered shocking ignorance in people who are part of his or her child's education. At the same time, we cannot think of many white parents of adopted black or other children or color who have not remarked on the helpful and supportive role of others in navigating the many contours and challenges that arise.

Things to consider

- *Race is an ever-present factor in all aspects of a child's education.* Much of what goes on related to race in school settings is invisible to white students, white parents, and many white teachers and other school personnel. Parents of children of color need to learn how to be aware of how race shows up in education.

- *Where children of color attend school has implications for both their education and their peer culture.* There is no easy answer to how white parents of children of color balance the trade-offs that unfortunately exist in many places between school quality and community diversity, but awareness is critical.

- *To understand a school or school district, it's important for white parents of children of color to do their own independent research and not simply take what they are told or what's printed on a web page.* It's important for parents to know as much as possible about the factors that will impact a child's trajectory in school, including racial mix of students, faculty, and administration; percent of students who go on to college; performance on state examinations for students overall and for student groups organized by racial category.

- *School curricula and lessons continue to under- and misrepresent people of color.* Be aware, ask questions, make suggestions, and do not settle for answers like, "We do as much as we can." If the curriculum has holes or the assignments are insensitive to either race or adoption, it's time to "be in the face" of teachers and others in charge of what happens at school.

- *Unless you live in a "minority majority" community, your child of color is likely to be spotlighted, erased, or both.* Keep the communication channels between you and your child of color open about experiences like this, even if your child seems not to want to talk about it.

- *Remember, education is the most powerful resource any person has.* Your job as a parent is to be attentive to how race affects that resource and to be willing to be an advocate and to join in alliance with others when problems arise.

References

Carter, D. J. (2008) "On Spotlighting and Ignoring Racial Group Members in the Classroom." In M. Pollock (ed.) *Everyday Antiracism: Getting Real about Race in School.* New York: The New Press. Available through Southern Poverty Law Center, "Teaching Tolerance Project" Available at www.tolerance.org/tdsi/sites/tolerance.org.tdsi/files/assets/general/TDSI_Carter.pdf, accessed on 7 February 2013.

Feistritzer, C.M. (2011) "Profiles of Teachers in the U.S. 2011." Washington D.C.: National Center for Education Information. Available at www.edweek.org/media/pot2011final-blog.pdf, accessed on 7 February 2013.

Fishman, F. and Harrington, E.S. (2007) "School Issues and Adoption: Academic Considerations and Adaptation." In R.A. Javier, A.L. Baden, F.A. Biafora and Camacho-Gingerich, A. (eds) *Handbook of Adoption: Implications for Researchers, Practitioners, and Families.* Thousand Oaks, CA: Sage.

Irvine, J. T. and Gal, S. (1999) "Language Ideology and Linguistic Differentiation." In P.V. Kroskrity (ed.) *Regimes of Language—Ideologies, Polities, and Identities.* Santa Fe, NM: School of American Research Press.

Julian, T. (2012) "Work-life earnings by field of degree and occupation for people with a Bachelor's degree: 2011." *American Community Survey Briefs.* Washington, D.C.: U.S. Census Bureau. Available at www.census.gov/prod/2012pubs/acsbr11-04.pdf, accessed on 7 February 2013.

Landsman, J. (2004) "Confronting the racism of low expectations." *Closing Achievement Gap 62,* 3, 28–32. Available at www.e3smallschools.org/documents/ConfrontingtheRacismofLowExpectations.pdf, accessed on 7 February 2013.

Landsman, J. (2009) *A White Teacher Talks about Race.* Lanham, MD: Roman and Littlefield [originally published in 2001 by Scarecrow Press].

National Center for Education Statistics (2012). *Digest of Education Statistics.* Available at http://nces.ed.gov/programs/digest/d12/tables/dt12_068.asp, accessed on 21 June 2013.

Sanchez, C. (2012) "Firestorm erupts over Virginia's education goals." National Public Radio. 12 Novmeber. Available at www.npr.org/2012/11/12/163703499/firestorm-erupts-over-virginia-s-education-goals, accessed on 7 February 2013.

Snyder, C. R. (2012) "Racial socialization in cross-racial families." *Journal of Black Psychology 38,* 2, 228–253.

Resources

Coates, Rodney (2011) "Covert Racism in an Age of Color Blindness!" *This Week in Sociology,* 12 October. Available at *www.thisweekinsociology.com/2011/10/covert-racism-in-age-of-color-blindness.html.*

This opinion piece deals with the underside of what is often called "post-racial society"—the subtle forms of racism that continue to underlie language and cultural practices, and that are experienced most directly by "racial non-elites."

Great Schools Staff. "Private Versus Public." Available at *www.greatschools.org/find-a-school/defining-your-ideal/59-private-vs-public-schools.gs*.

This short article offers a brief overview of information about private schools, such as admissions, cost, class size, and special needs. Navigate through the posted ads to get this two page article. Information about private schools is also available on the websites for The National Association of Independent Schools, which is available at *www.nais.org/Pages/default.aspx* and the Council for American Private Education, which is available at *www.capenet.org*.

Rich, M. (2012) "For young Latino readers, an image is missing." *The New York Times*, 3 December, p.A1(L).

The focus of this article in on the scarcity of Latino/a characters in books for young children, but Rich also highlights the overall problem and lack of diversity in the books that children are exposed to in the classroom. The author notes that some textbook companies do better than publishers of the various story series that are popular with children.

Traywick, LaVona and Marshall, James P. "Tips for talking with teachers." Available at *www.uaex.edu/Other_Areas/publications/PDF/FSFCS207.pdf*.

This article from the Family and Consumer Sciences department at the University of Arkansas contains some sound advice and practical guidance for how to talk with teachers in a range of situations, from scheduling conferences to communication initiated by a teacher about your child.

CHAPTER 6

Creating a Support System for You and Your Child—

"It Takes a Village"

In 1996, Hillary Clinton published *It Takes a Village: And Other Lessons Children Teach Us*. Taken from an African proverb, the title was meant to imply that children need resources and support not only from their parents but also from people and institutions beyond their immediate families. Then in his acceptance speech at the Republic National Convention that year, Senator Bob Dole, the party's nominee for President of the U.S., said, "I am here to tell you, it does not take a village to raise a child. It takes a family to raise a child" (Dole 1996, para21). Well, we are here to tell white parents of children of color that it does take a village to raise a child of color.

We are not saying that family is unimportant. In fact, family is critical and central to a child's development, feeling of security, and overall well-being. Family provides a child with love, stability, discipline, financial support, a foundation for values and personal identity, and encouragement. In Chapter 3, we stressed that a child's identity is forged in his or her family, and that identity is central to the child's development. For a child of color, however, that family identity is not the only identity that will be important. To repeat a point from Chapter 1—"race matters." Children of color need to learn how to negotiate a world in which an identity may be imposed on them by other people, an identity that bears history and that differs from the one they and their family have created for themselves. White adoptive parents need support to help their children learn how to negotiate that world. They also need help in the many practical issues that we've detailed throughout the book—choosing a community in which to live, dealing with doctors and teachers who aren't knowledgeable about people of their children's race, finding a beauty salon or barbershop, discovering welcoming and comfortable vacation spots for their family. Finally white parents of children of color need support for themselves as they encounter the many challenges they will face. The village it takes is one of many regions, each important for parents and children alike. The village supports, nourishes, and enlivens how we live our lives.

In this chapter we offer suggestions for building the village that will nurture and sustain you and your child throughout your adoption journey.

Family, friends, and acquaintances— *"Whom do I know?"*

Sometimes you can begin to build your village with help from family and friends. We were lucky to be part of an interracial family with Korean, Chinese, and Hawaiian heritage even before we adopted our sons. That meant that our children would have several biracial cousins to turn to or at least use as reference points as they were growing up, and we would have the experiences of Fern's siblings and their spouses to help guide us. We also had several close black friends who advised us from the very start of our journey. Not all of them were convinced initially that we were doing the right thing by adopting a black child. One friend expressed concern that we didn't fully understand how much we would need to teach our child about racism, and all of them told us they would be watching closely to make sure that we kept our child's hair properly. They all expressed support for us regardless of our decision, offered to give us advice and suggestions when they were needed, and served as honorary "aunties" and "uncles" (as did many of our white friends).

Our immediate circle of family and friends wasn't sufficient, however, to fill all of the places in our village. Both of our immediate families lived halfway across the country. Visits in both directions gave our sons a strong sense of family ties, but didn't give us day-to-day support. All parents have to reach out to acquaintances and relative strangers to help them find sitters for their children for an evening out together or when a child is ill and the parent has to go to work, but adoptive parents have to reach out for help in meeting the additional challenges they face. When we began our adoption search, we knew very little about the adoption process. We contacted numerous adoption agencies but knew no one who had recently adopted a child and could help us negotiate the process. And we didn't know any whites who had adopted a child of color. So we reached out to strangers. When Marlene read a story in *The Boston Globe* about a single woman who had adopted a child from Colombia, she tracked her down and called her. The woman gladly talked with her about her adoption process. Both of us asked everyone we knew and those we met if they knew people we could talk with who had adopted a child of color. As we contacted more and more people (often feeling anxious about intruding on those we didn't know), we began to build a network of resources that we could continue to turn to after we adopted our sons. No one said "no."

In our experience, we have found that people generally like to help other people. And adoptive parents particularly like to help other adoptive parents and prospective adoptive parents—they remember how grateful they were for the help and advice they received. When both friends and strangers learned we were writing this book, they would give us names of their friends or relatives who had adopted children of color and offer to introduce us to them. When our older son was just two months old, we spent one day hiking with friends on Monhegan Island off the coast of Maine, carrying our son in a back carrier. There were few people on the island that day. At one point we encountered a white man and woman in their 50s who stared at us and then started walking closer toward us. Not knowing what to expect, we felt tense, not sure what they wanted. The man put his hand in his pocket, withdrew his wallet, pulled out a photograph, and handed it to us. It was a photograph of a young African American man. The man and woman smiled and he said, "We started awhile ago." We stopped and chatted with them, happy to meet parents who had already pursued the path we had just embarked on. Closer to home, one of Fern's colleagues and his wife had adopted an African American boy as an infant who was now a high school student. Another had adopted a Korean child when she was about four years old. They were a source of constant support throughout our adoption process and as our children grew.

As you look for the people to populate your village, remember to reach out to new acquaintances and even to strangers. You have to be willing to be proactive in making contacts and initiating new friendships. That includes reaching out to people of color and having the "difficult dialogues" that Marsha Houston describes between whites and blacks (see Chapter 1 for more information). We learned that it's important also to listen not only for support but for corrective advice—suggestions for how to proceed that may differ from your own instincts.

Meet new people—*"Whom do I need to know?"*

Although we often have some resources in our immediate circle of friends and family, most of us live relatively insular lives spending time with people who are like us. Marlene does an exercise with her students in which she asks them to imagine they were home for the weekend and had a party; they write down the names of the 20 people they would invite to the party. Invariably, the students, even those who say they have a wide circle of friends of diverse backgrounds, select mostly people of their own racial and ethnic background. The U.S. is racially diverse but most Americans have family and friendship circles that are relatively homogeneous. This may be changing somewhat among young people, but it's still the case that "birds of a feather flock together." That homogeneity means that white adoptive parents of children of color need to reach out to new people to help build the village that will support them and their children. Sometimes it seems artificial to pursue a person who is a stranger or only an acquaintance, but the more people in your village, the fuller your lives will be. It's important, however, not to take advantage of others. We have heard many people of color—especially African Americans—comment about how tired they get of *teaching whites* about race. Yet, we have found that most people of color will be supportive and helpful, especially when children are involved. What's central is that your contacts are not simply need-based but also convey a genuine interest and appreciation for the help you are given.

Online communities and resources

One way to reach out is through online adoption resource sites, communities, and blogs. These will provide quick and easy access both to information and to other parents who are facing similar issues. You can scan previous discussions about topics, post questions, and add your own insights to ongoing discussions.

Increasingly, a wealth of information is available online about adoption, and some of these resources contain content related to adopting across race. Here we highlight some of the main sites and resources currently available, but you will be able to find more specialized information on your own. Remember, however, that the content on these sites changes all of the time, and new sites are added almost daily. When you are searching for information on your own, we also caution you to check into the ownership of the sites that you find. The topic of interracial adoption is rife with political and religious implications that give rise to particular points of view about families, children, adoption, etc. Knowing the political and/or religious positions of the site owners and writers is important as you assess the relevance of the information to your situation. At the same time, there may be useful information and resources through a website that is not aligned with your own religion or politics.

One gateway to a range of resources can be found at www. adoption.org. This site, which is owned by Adoption Media, LLC, includes articles on various topics, blogs, current news about adoption, and *Adoption E-Magazine*. For example, information can be found on trends in international adoption (including statistics by year and country from the U.S. Department of State), on legislation that exists concerning transracial adoption, as well as links to various blogs on specific topics. Another useful source is the North American Council on Adoptable Children. This organization sponsors a magazine, *Adoptalk*, which is available online (www.nacac.org/ adoptalk/adoptalk.html), and a database of parent resources and support groups organized by subject and state (www.nacac. org/parentgroups/database.html). A more policy, advocacy, and research-oriented resource is provided by the Evan B. Donaldson Adoption Institute (www.adoptioninstitute.org/index.php). To find online adoption communities, see adoption.about. com, which is an adoption and foster care site that includes numerous online adoption communities (adoption.about.com/

od/onlinecommunities/Adoption_Online_Communities.htm).
We found no interracial adoption communities on this website
when we looked in September 2012, but one or more may exist
by now. The site also provides instructions for starting your
own online adoption community, so you could look for other
adoptive parents interested in discussing interracial adoption
issues by creating your own community on the site. Finally, by
simply googling "adoption blogs," you can find a wide range
of interesting resources—many of them focused on personal
stories and others more broadly defined.

As adopted children grow older, they will often seek
out information by themselves on the internet, blogs, online
communities, and contacts online through social networks such
as Facebook. Like many aspects of children's lives—especially
as children reach adolescence—parents are not always aware of
these initiatives. It's a good idea to ask your children whenever
it seems a natural part of the conversation if they have been
learning about adoption, multiracial families, or race on their
own and if you can be helpful in any way. Even if your children
reject your offer to help, they will still know you are aware that
they may have questions about adoption in general and their
birth families and/or adoption story in particular, and you will
be reinforcing the message that you are available to talk with
them and help them if they change their mind. All young people
struggle to make sense of their experiences as they are growing
up and most tend to do so on their own. It is important for
them to know, however, that you are always there to help them
through that struggle if they decide they need help.

Adoption groups

Online resources are very helpful for parents. They do not,
however, provide enough support for your family. To ensure
that your children don't feel isolated and alone and to give them
opportunities to meet other children in families similar to theirs,

you need to find similar families. You can do this in a variety of ways. Dalton (2002) suggests a broad range of possibilities from playgroups to formalized organizations.

Many adoption agencies have yearly or sometimes even more frequent get-togethers for families who adopted through their agency. Often these gatherings are specifically for families with children adopted from a particular country or region of the world, or domestic adoptions of children of color, or some other particular group. Other times they are for all families who adopted through that agency. Many gatherings will be focused on speaker events, family outings, and such. Whether general or particular, however, gatherings of adoptive families give you and your children an opportunity to meet other parents and children in family configurations similar to yours. You can choose to maintain your relationship with some or many of the families that attend simply by seeing them each year, or perhaps more often, at each gathering. Or you could develop a closer relationship with one or more families, setting up play dates for your children with them or having the parents and children come for lunch or dinner, or join your family on an outing. Depending on where you live, you may have to drive some distance to attend adoption events, but we think it's worth the time it takes. We met several families this way who became close friends.

Some adoptive parents also have the option to enroll their children in a cultural school or in extra-curricular activities that allow the children to learn about their birth cultures. Friends with children adopted from China and Korea send their children to Chinese or Korean cultural school. Other friends have enrolled their children in language classes in the native language of their child's culture. We know of one family of white parents and adopted Chinese children where the parents learned Chinese (studying it for many years) and traveled to China every year with their children. These options provide numerous opportunities for you and your children to meet other families with similar backgrounds and interests. In some cases you will meet parents and children who share a particular culture, for example, a Chinese American family. In these instances you have the opportunity to create a friendship across differences in cultural backgrounds because you share cultural interests. Such a friendship offers access to a wealth of cultural knowledge and understanding and gives your children access to people with whom they share some commonality. In other instances, you will meet interracial families similar to yours, giving your children an opportunity to see families similar to theirs.

Although attending adoption agency gatherings or enrolling your children in language and culture courses will help create your village, some parents may want to have access to a more consistent and enduring group of families. We chose to form our own adoption group with other families similar to ours. Such a group can take a variety of shapes. We describe here three possible types of groups.

GROUP 1—*"MY FAMILY IS LIKE YOURS"*

Create a small group of adoptive families with parents and children similar to yours. Keep the number of families relatively small so that you can more easily coordinate schedules and be able to attend sporting events, concerts, plays, or other events; celebrate holidays; and even vacation together. Establish a regular meeting schedule, perhaps one meeting every season, and plan family activities that will engage parents and children. Create some annual events that the children will anticipate every year, for example, a summer outing to the beach or a camping trip. Include one or more events that are culturally appropriate for your families such as an annual Kwanzaa celebration, attendance at a Martin Luther King Birthday breakfast, an outing to a black musical performance (such as Boston's annual *Black Nativity*), participation in a Cinco de Mayo or a Chinese New Year celebration. As the children get older, adjust the activities to their interests. It will be important to be vigilant about scheduling these events and to make sure these are a PRIORITY for you and your family.

GROUP 2—*"OTHER FAMILIES HAVE
KIDS WHO LOOK LIKE ME"*

Create a large group of adoptive families with children who share a cultural heritage. Have parents and children meet together once or twice each year so that children have an opportunity to get to know one another and see families similar to theirs. Use the group primarily, however, as a resource for parents. Parents can meet more often throughout the year to talk about particular issues they encounter, sharing their stories and generating ideas for responding to different situations. Because the group is large, parents might decide to meet in smaller groups with other parents who are facing similar issues or be in contact through e-mail or Facebook. The group gatherings that include children could focus on a cultural celebration that reflects the children's shared cultural heritage, but they might also simply be activities that children at various ages might enjoy.

GROUP 3—*"MY FAMILY IS SORT OF LIKE YOURS"*

Create a group of adoptive families with children who have varied cultural backgrounds. The group can be large or small, but the focus is on activities for children and parents together. The activities center primarily on discovering and celebrating the children's different cultural heritages. These children and parents learn to appreciate their cultural differences but also come to see the things they share—loving families, parents who are concerned about their children's emotional and intellectual development, parents and children who may face different degrees of discrimination, and, of course, adoption as a way to create a family. Activities for younger children might include projects they can work on together. Older children might be more interested in movies that feature particular cultural backgrounds. Groups formed by a diverse range of families often begin in religious or other organizational settings. For example, we were part of an informal multiracial and multicultural group of families in our synagogue; some of the couples were mixed race, and some of the children were adopted.

There are many variations of each of these groups. We chose to become part of a small group of white same-sex couples who had adopted African American or biracial (African American and Hispanic) children. We kept the group small (six families) so that both parents and children would have a chance to create deeper and more personal relationships with each other. As we have described in previous chapters, we met at least four times each year as a group, usually at one family's home (we rotated homes throughout the year). When the group started, the children ranged in age from one year old to several weeks old. Over the years, the families adopted more children. We celebrated Kwanzaa together each December, camped by the seashore each summer (sometimes in the rain—remember vigilance in scheduling), attended various musical events together, and as the children got older, celebrated high school and college graduations and, at this point in time, one wedding and the birth of two babies. Although the "children" no longer see each other as a group, they continue to be connected through Facebook. The parents get together in various groupings for dinner, to attend a concert or sporting event, or engage in some other activity. Our conversations are far ranging but always include discussing our children.

Conclusion—*"Who's got my back?"*

We recently sat down to talk with one of the couples in our adoption group about this book. Each of the women had read a chapter in the book and we were talking about the different ways friends and family members had responded over the years to our interracial families. As we talked about our experiences and how we had handled them, one of the women said, "You know, there were many times when I'm sure that other people handled them for us. Other parents, for example, dealt with issues at school on our behalf. They always had our back." The conversation made us realize that there have been many people in our village who have been there for us throughout our journey and whose support and advocacy for us went unnoticed at the time. At the synagogue that we belonged to when the boys were young, the rabbi read the names of couples who were celebrating their wedding anniversary that week during the Friday evening service. Because we were not legally married, our names were not included. Unknown to us, several members of the congregation went to the rabbi and asked him to include us, arguing that our relationship and family should be recognized by the congregation. These were friends who either had adopted children or, in one case, were an interracial couple with two biological children. We were surprised and pleased when our names were read several weeks later. We learned many months later from the rabbi that he had been approached by others on our behalf. There was also the situation we referred to in Chapter 5 when one of our sons was denied a home-stay when his high school band visited Japan. His white friend stepped up to be his ally and to stay with him in the hostel, and we learned later that this boy's parents had discussed this not only with their son but with other band parents. We know there were other times when we were helped by others, but there is no way to know exactly when or by whom.

When the Massachusetts Supreme Judicial Court ruled that it was unconstitutional to disallow same-sex marriage and the state legislature declined to pass legislation prohibiting same-sex marriage, we were not initially going to get married. We had been together over 27 years at that point, our employers had long ago granted us joint health insurance benefits, and the lack of federal recognition of same-sex marriage meant that we could still not receive any of the tax benefits accorded to married couples. Our sons, however, convinced us otherwise—primarily because they wanted to have a big party to celebrate. Our wedding was simple. With the boys as our witnesses, we were married by the town clerk in the town where the boys attended school. To our surprise, the next morning we received flowers and gifts from the parents of several of their friends. Parents we knew but not well. When we asked the boys how these people knew we had gotten married, they said they had told all of their friends. We were touched by the gifts and the support they expressed. We also realized that there were many people in the community, some of whom we didn't know personally, who were there for us, not only at this moment but most likely many times before, standing up for us when teachers, children, other parents, or even friends had said something derogatory about our family. We realized that there were probably teachers who had made different decisions about an assignment or about a curricular change because they knew our family. While we were writing this book, we thought back to times when comments from white teachers signaled to us that they had been there for our children, knowing that they had to deal everyday with their "difference." We realized that we were lucky to live in a community where so many people, known and unknown, supported our family. But we also realized that many people live in such communities. We have learned over the course of our adoption journey that there are many good people out there, some of whom understand racial prejudice and others who are willing to learn about it, and all of whom will work to combat it. We wish you success in building your village and joy throughout your adoption experience.

Things to consider

- *No person (or family) is an island.* You and your child need support from family, friends, and other members of the community.

- *Don't be afraid to ask for help, even from people you don't know.* Be willing to reach out to new people and to build new friendships.

- *Use online resources.* Seek out information and contacts online, but be sure that you check for any hidden agendas.

- *Form your own adoption group or join an existing group.* Make the group and its activities a priority for you and your family.

References

Clinton, H. (1996) *It Takes a Village: And Other Lessons Children Teach Us.* New York: Simon & Schuster.

Dalton, J.M. (2002) "How to Start a Parent Support Group." *Adoptive Families.* Available at http://adoptivefamilies.com/articles.php?aid=451, accessed on 7 February 2013.

Dole, B. (1996) "Bob Dole's Acceptance Speech." 15 August. Available at www.pbs.org/newshour/convention96/floor_speeches/bob_dole.html, accessed on 7 February 2013.

Index

academic achievement 130–3
ADHD (Attention Deficit
    Hyperactivity Disorder) 54
adolescence 77–8, 107–10, 128, 155
Adoption Foundation 22
Adoption Institute 154
Adoption Media, LLC 154
adoption process
    application forms 19–20
    group sessions 20
    home study 24, 30, 49
    need for clarity 31
    rejecting a referral 30–1
adoption support groups 80, 155–9
African American culture 38–9
    and identity 79
    incorporation into family 80–2, 84–8
    lack of knowledge of 42
    looking good as cultural value 89,
        91–2
    similarities and differences 43, 77
African American people
    children 19–21, 108
    income divide 37
    low expectations for 27–8, 64, 131–2
    media representation 96
    quality of life 36
    skin condition 92–3
    vacation spot 94
Agiesta, J. 32
Ahuja, G. 37–8
Aladdin 87
"all blacks look alike" stereotype 64

American Anthropological Association
    33
application forms 19–20
articulation stereotype 76
Aryan race 33
Asian culture 77
Asian stereotypes 39, 62, 77, 96, 113
Asian, use of term 15, 16
aspirations 27–8
assumptions
    cultural 14, 79, 112
    in schools 135–7
athleticism stereotype 55, 58, 138

bar mitzvahs 82
barbers 90–2
Barbershop 91
baseball 88
Beauty Shop 91
Big Brothers Big Sisters 95
biracial
    couples, questions asked of 60
    use of term 16
birth parents 51–2, 68, 104, 105–6,
    107–10
black families, experience of 130
black hair and skin 89–93
black men as violent stereotype 77, 117
black men, fear of and fear for 24, 26
Black Nativity 158
black-on-black violence 35
black story characters 85–6
black, use of term 16, 73

blacks, targeting of 26, 35, 36, 56–7, 78, 117
blogs 154–5
blue collar workers 27
books 85–6
Boston, Massachusetts 25–6
Bowman, B.B. 117
boys, stereotypes 23–4
Brooks, Gwendolyn 82
Brown, S. 70
bullying 143
Byrd, A. 98

Callahan, N.M. 119
candor, need for 48, 59
Carter, D.J. 134
Census report 36, 37
Centers for Disease Control and Prevention 54
cerebral palsy 18–19
charter schools 127
children, communication with
    about adoption 101–10
    about background 51–2
    about race 110–17
    clear and frank 68
    levels of understanding 100
child's background
    caution about discussing 51
    eagerness to discuss 51
    "history belongs to the child" 52, 68, 69
    planning responses to queries 50
    questions about 49–50, 59–60
    sharing information with child 51–2
    see also birth parents
Chinese Americans 39, 156–7
Chinese stereotypes 62
    see also Asian stereotypes
Christmas 81, 84–5
church 91–2
city life 26, 79
clarity, need for 31
classical music concert experience 112
Clinton, H. 149
Coates, R. 147
cognitive growth 30–1
Cohen, S.A. 36

colleges 27–8, 64–5, 126–7, 146
Colombia 19, 109, 151
communication
    about adoption across race 47–9
    about child's background 49–52, 67–8
    adoption as taboo subject 101
    between black and white women 42–3
    with black friends 47–8, 139
    with children 68, 100–17
    responding to racist comments 52–65
    responding to unwanted praise 65–7
communities 25–9, 124–5, 153–5
Confucianism 39
Coretta Scott King Award 63
Cracking the Codes: the System of Racial Inequity 46
Crawford, Carl 35
Cuckens, B. 70
cultural separation 42–3
cultural similarities 43
cultural spaces 91–2
cultural tourism 85
"culture keeping" 82–3, 85
cultures
    incorporation into family 79–97
    racially-linked 38–43
curriculum
    advantages of private school 128
    limited in presenting history 136, 140–1, 143
    as source of institutional racism 62–3, 131–2, 136–7, 142, 146

Dalton, J.M. 156
dance troupe concert experience 111–12
Daniel, G.R. 59
Database of Award-Winning Children's Literature 63
Davis, O. 115–16
day care choices 125
"Dear Margo" 100
defensiveness 75–7, 97
Denton, N. 46
developmental stages
    of racial identity 73–8
    in understanding adoption 102–10

"difficult dialogues" 42–3, 152
dinner conversations 88, 111
Disney films 86–7
diversity
    and educational quality 124, 127,
        128
    in schools 62–3, 142
dog ownership analogy 99–100
Dole, B. 149
dolls 38, 114–15
Donaldson, Evan B. 154
Driving While Black report 56
Dumbo 86
DWB ("driving while black") 36, 55–7

early childhood education 124–5
educational stereotypes 64–5, 131–2
Elton John 23
English language 115–16
environment 25–9, 44, 123–5, 146
erasure 133–5, 146
ethnicity, use of term 15–16
expectations, lower 27–8, 61–2, 130–3,
    142–3
experience, lack of 139

Facebook 155, 158, 159
family, friends and acquaintances 47–8,
    150–2
family, importance of 149–50
family reactions 21–2, 47
family trees 135–6, 141
Feistritzer, C.M. 129
films 86–7
Fishman, F. 125, 141
flexibility 44
Fryklund, K. 64
Furnish, David 23

Gal, S. 134
gender 22–4
gender roles 27, 37
Gerson, M. 24
"ghetto" 96
girls, preference for 22–4
"good people/lucky children" dynamic
    65–7, 69
guidance, lack of 18, 151

guidance summaries 32, 44, 68–9, 97,
    117–18, 145–6, 162
guilt 76–7

hair 77–8, 89–93, 115, 125
Harrell, E. 35
Harrington, E.S. 125, 141
Henry, M.J. 46, 101
Herbert, B. 24
Hispanic people
    birth parents 108–9
    ethnic cultures 39
    stereotypes 39, 64, 96, 131–2
history lessons 62–3, 74–5, 87–8,
    108–9, 135–7
Hitler, Adolf 33
Hofheimer Bettmann, E. 70
home preparation 83–7
home study 24, 30, 49
homicide 24
Hooda, S. 24
hooks, bell 133
Houston, M. 42, 152
Hughes, Langston 82
Hughey, M.W. 46

identity
    expression of 77–8, 113
    family 149–50
    gender role 36–7
    personal 72
    racial *see* racial identity
images and objects of culture, dearth
    of 84–5
"in group" 55, 91
incarceration 24
income disparity 36, 37, 108
India 18–19
information sharing
    about child's background 49–52
    with children 101–10
    deciding on degree of 105, 106
institutional racism 36–7, 62–3, 131–2,
    136–7
internalized racism 37–8, 93, 113
interpersonal racism 34–6
interracial adoption, use of term 14
Irvine, J.T. 134

isolation, feelings of 106–7
It Takes a Village: And Other Lessons Children Teach Us 149
Italy, experience in 17

Jacobson, H. 83
Japan trip experience 138–9, 160
Jewish people 81–2, 134
John, Elton 23
Julian, T. 129
Jungle Book, The 86

Karenga, Maulana 80
Keefer, B. 51, 52, 119
Korea 18, 156
Krueger, A. 70
Kwanzaa party 80–1, 159

Lam, A. 98
Landsman, J. 131–2, 142–3
language, use of 115–16
laser hair removal 93
Latino/a
    scarcity of characters in books 148
    stereotypes 64–5, 77, 131–2
    use of term 16
Lazare, Louise 133
Lazarre, J. 46
laziness stereotype 35, 39, 61–2, 77
learning opportunities 87–8
lesbian and gay adoption 18, 23, 80, 107
libraries 63
Lion King, The 86
Lipsky, S. 37
literal descriptions 73–4
location 25–9, 44, 123–5, 146
looking good 89, 91–2
"lucky children" concept 65–7, 132
lynching 34

magnet schools 127
marriage 18, 160–1
Marshall, J.P. 148
Martin, Trayvon 34, 78
Maslowski, J. 70
Massachusetts 18, 24, 25–6, 94, 124, 160

Massey, D. 46
McGuire, T.G. 36
McIntosh, P. 39, 40, 55
media representation 28, 96, 131
meeting new people 153
Melina, L. 102, 104, 107
mentoring 95
Miranda, J. 36
mixed race, use of term 16
"Monday" 35
multiracial, use of term 16

NABSW (National Association of Black Social Workers) 19–20, 48
names 115
National Center for Education Statistics 127–8
neighborhoods 25–6, 28–9, 92, 124–5
Nelson, J. 94
New Normal, The 107
Norris, M. 89
North American Council on Adoptable Children 154

Obama, Barak 28, 32, 98, 111
online communities and resources 153–5
open adoption 101–2
openness to change 44
operational thinking 74–5
order of racial preference 58

parental involvement in schools 140–4
Parks, G.S. 46
Passover story 81–2
peers 130
personal space 115
Peru 19
Peterson, E. 36
Philippines 18
physical characteristics
    issues related to 115
    seeing race as set of 73–4, 113
police 26, 35, 36, 56–7, 78, 117
politics and race 88
Pollack, D. 46, 101
post-racial society 32, 147
praise, unwanted 65–7

prejudice
  defensiveness about 75–6
  hidden 21
  understanding of 74, 75
preschool choices 125
preschool experiences 60, 74, 115
Princess and the Frog, The 86–7
private schools 127–9, 148
profiling 36, 56, 78

Quintana, S. 73, 74, 77
Quiroz, P.A. 85

race
  as artificial category system 31, 33
  an ever-present factor 145
  talking to children about 110–17
  in U.S. society 32–3
  use of term 14–15
"race matters" 22, 29, 32–3, 44, 97,
    118, 150
racial awareness, developing 110–11
racial genocide 19, 48
racial identity 71–2
  development of 72–8
  incorporation into family 79–97
racial riots 34–5
racial thinking 59–60, 145
racially-linked cultures 38–43
racism
  responses to 59–65, 69
  responsibility to teach children about
    78
  types of 34–8
rap culture 96
"redlining" 34
rejecting a referral 30–1
religious celebrations 80–2
researching schools 126–7
residence, suitable *see* environment
Rice, C. 113
Rich, M. 148
Roach, J. 33
Robinson, Jackie 88
role models 95–7
Ross, S. 32
Rothstein, R. 37
Rupp, L. 70

Sanchez, C. 131
school activities 138–9
school assignments 135–7
  see also history lessons
Schooler, J.E. 51, 52, 119
schools 121–3, 144–5
  academic achievement 130–3
  in Boston 25–6
  deciding on 123–30
  help from parents 140–4
  need for vigilance in 61–2
  questions for 143
  responding to unfair treatment
    133–9
Sege, I. 94
self-regard 113–14
Sesame Street 86
Shapiro, T.M. 37
sickle-cell anemia 33
Siegel, D.H. 101
skin care 92
skin color 21
  desire to change 92–3
  and early development stage 73–4
  questions about 52–3
slavery 33, 36–7, 74–5, 81–2, 135–6,
    137, 140
slippage 145
Smith, S.L. 101
Snyder, C.R. 123
social class 75, 108–9, 112, 118
social cognition 75–6
social networks 155
Social Security office experience 41
Song of the South 86
Spanish-speaking stereotype 64
Spickard, P. 59
spotlighting 133–5, 146
Staples, B. 56
stereotypes
  "all blacks look alike" 64
  articulation 76
  Asians are good at math 39, 62, 77,
    113
  athleticism 55, 58, 138
  black men as violent 77, 117
  educational 64–5, 131–2
  of girls and boys 23–4

stereotypes *cont.*
    Hispanic 39, 64, 96, 131–2
    laziness 35, 39, 61–2, 77
    in media 96
    negative 35–6
    social class 108–9
    Spanish-speaking 64
Stern-LaRosa, C. 70
stories
    adoption 102–3, 104–5
    black characters in 85–6
    importance of 67–8, 69
sub-Saharan populations 33
suburbs, life in 25–7, 126, 132
sun screen 92
support systems 149–50
    adoption groups 80, 155–9
    family, friends and acquaintances
        150–2
    help from unexpected sources
        159–61
    meeting new people 153
    online communities and resources
        153–5
SWB ("shopping while black") 55–6

talking *see* communication
Tatum, B. 98
teachers
    assessments of ability 61–2, 130–3
    of color, scarcity 129
    communicating concerns to 63,
        74–5, 137, 141, 146
    singling out, spotlighting and erasure
        133–5
teenagers 77–8, 107–10, 128, 155
television shows 86, 96
terminology 14–16
Tharps, L. 98
"The Talk" 116–17
Tompkins, S. 103
transracial adoption, use of term 14
Traywick, L. 148
Tulsa, Oklahoma 34

unemployment rate 24
U.S. Bureau of the Census 15

vacations 93–4
verbal racism 35
vigilance, importance of 60–2, 114

West, C. 22
white privilege 39–41, 55, 56, 76, 84,
    97, 139
Wiley, K. 57
Wilkerson, I. 119
Wilson, Joe 111
women, as driving force behind
    adoption 22–3

Yancy, C.W. 36

Zimmerman, George 34